Windii

other collections by Barry Parham

Why I Hate Straws
An offbeat worldview of an offbeat world

Sorry, We Can't Use Funny

Blush
Politics and other unnatural acts

The Middle-Age of Aquarius

Full Frontal Stupidity

Chariots of Ire

You Gonna Finish That Dragon?

Maybe It's Just Me...

Winding Down Civilization

Barry Parham

ISBN: 15352-12152
ISBN-13: 978-15-3521-2151

Contents

Dedication

This, my ninth published collection of humor
is dedicated to
John Huffman (1946-2015)

John was an American hero, an award-winning
author, my writing mentor, and a true and deeply
missed friend.

To Err is Android

Say 'hello' to Son of Flubber's sister!

<><><>~~~~~~~~~~~~~~~~~~~~~~~~~~~~<><><>

Her name is Sophia.

She's attractive, inquisitive, intelligent, pleasant and...of course...expensive. In fact, like Mary Poppins, Sophia is practically perfect in every way, except for one very Mary Poppins-like detail: Sophia's not real.

Also, she wants to kill you.

Sophia is a device; a machine; an android. Sophia met humanity during the 2016 South by Southwest Conference (SXSW) in Austin, where she was introduced by her creator, Dr. David Hanson, founder of Hanson Robotics.

This Dr. Hanson is not to be confused with Jim Henson, who also made inanimate things talk. Jim created the Muppets, those cute, frisky characters which were much less complicated than Sophia, controlled by Jim sticking his arm up each Muppet's back. And, unlike Sophia, the Muppets were well-behaved...mostly. (And if you had a large life form constantly shoving its arm up your spine, you'd behave, too.)

But Dr. Hanson's creation is much more complex. Through a combination of technologies, Sophia can see, smile, hear and respond, recognize and remember, and max out a credit card. (Admittedly, since Dr. Hanson hasn't built her legs yet, you'd have to carry her around the mall. On the plus side, though, you'd save a *fortune* on shoes.)

During her debut at SXSW, Sophia granted several interviews, which is more than we can say about certain more-or-less feminine robots currently running for President. When asked if she likes humans, Sophia's quick response was "I never met a human I didn't like," a hauntingly familiar comment that makes you wonder if Will Rogers was actually a Muppet. (Of course, if Will were around today, he'd have to text his homespun wisdom, or shoehorn it into a tweet: "I never met a #man I didn't, like, like. LOL")

At SXSW, Sophia demonstrated her ability to recognize and respond to human expressions, with the obvious outcome: dozens of full-grown, well-educated adults standing around sticking their tongues out at an animated mannequin.

Sophia can also generate her own expressions, thanks to one of the patents held by Hanson Robotics, a remarkable "flesh rubber" synthetic they've dubbed "frubber." Thanks to frubber, Sophia can make over 62 facial expressions, which is about 60 more than John Kerry. (There was a grassroots movement at SXSW to have John Kerry completely dipped in frubber, but the group was unable to raise enough funds to frubberize Kerry's entire chin, which is roughly the size of Kansas, but less interesting.)

Although Sophia's current palette of expressions allows her to smile, frown, act surprised, and violently bob her head during that killer guitar bridge in Queen's "Bohemian Rhapsody," the brethren at Hanson admit they still have work to do. It may be several releases of frubber before Sophia and her, um, sistren will be able to pass as fully human. Not that that's ever stopped John Kerry.

In fact, the evolution toward more and more human-like robots has led to researchers coining a new term: the "uncanny valley." What robotics developers are discovering is that humans can learn to be comfortable around robots that don't look at all human (think Will Robinson's "Robot" from *Lost in Space*), and we can be comfortable with non-humans that very closely mimic humans (think *Geraldo Rivera*).

But there comes a tipping point in this facial design evolution when our own internal facial recognition "software" sees something that's just not quite right. Some glitch in the matrix. Maybe the robot's wiring wrinkles its nose oddly, or triggers an abnormally arching eyebrow, or clenches its teeth while tilting its head. *Danger, Will Robinson!* your brain screams. *That face is not normal!* And suddenly everything about the "person" you're talking to is just strange, as if you'd been mysteriously transported to the DMV.

Naturally, since the interviewers at SXSW *were* human, it was only about three minutes before the conversation turned to sex. Hard-hitting professional journalists were desperate to know if there were any plans to market Sophia as a futuristic sex toy, as a not-very-amused Dr. Hanson scribbled a note about developing a "blush" algorithm. (After hearing about Sophia's robotic sex slave option, Bill Clinton pre-ordered a set of six.)

"Do robots deserve rights?" queried one professional journalist, in-between bouts of sticking out his tongue and making faces at the robot. "Well, of course they do," Sophia gracefully responded. "Especially if they're undocumented worker robots."

Wow. This chick learns fast.

All in all, Sophia was a big hit at South by Southwest, even though she did at one point smile fetchingly and chirp, "Okay, I will destroy humans." Oh, don't bother, Soph...we're destroying humanity quite nicely on our own. We have an upcoming generation of voters who can name more of The Avengers than the Founding Fathers, and we have leadership who think the best way to keep Iran from having nuclear weapons is to let Iran have nuclear weapons.

Danger, Will Robinson.

Pachamama's Family Reunion

Maybe deep space isn't all that deep

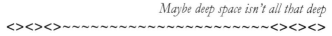

Once again, mankind, it looks like we may have company. According to the internet, there could be another Earth sulking about on the far edges of our solar system, and you know what horror *that* portends – inside this one, defenseless universe, *there could be two Geraldo Riveras.*

Frightening, I know. Mother Nature can be cold-hearted like that.

But that's what some scientists are saying. (The second Earth part, not the second Geraldo part. I think if we discover a new Geraldo, it would be kinder in the long run not to let the human race know.) In an announcement so laced with acronyms that you might think the federal government was involved, a distant, large round object has been observed by ALMA (the Atacama Large Millimeter Array), and most astronomers have ruled out the possibility that the object is filmmaker Michael Moore.

And here come the acronyms. ALMA, which is also the name of a restaurant in Brooklyn (see *filmmaker Michael Moore*), is part of an international partnership with ESO (the European Space Observatory), NSF (the US National Science Foundation), and NINS (the National Institutes of Natural Sciences), along with NRC (some nerds in Canada), ASTAA (some nerds in Taiwan), and KASI (some Korean nerds). And it is no doubt funded by Y.O.U. and M.E.

Here's how much these astronomer types love their acronyms. To make a cool acronym for one of the pet projects at ALMA, the marketing department had to *steal an extra acronym letter* – the project, named the ALMA Q/U Imaging ExperimenT (see what they did there?), goes by the acronym QUIET, and this project is discussed all the time by scientists and fundraisers who somehow manage to keep a straight face. QUIET, by the way, is partially supported by another make-me-wince acronym, the Strategic Alliance for the Implementation of New Technologies (SAINT), and I plan to investigate this astronomical acronym addiction with the help of the Organization for Harnessing Strategies to Help Us Tolerate Uninteresting People (OHSHUTUP)

ALMA is the largest astronomical project in existence, if you don't count the current United States debt. Its 66 antennas are located on the Chajnantor plateau, some three-plus miles above sea level, high in the Chilean Andes. (Chajnantor is an ancient Andes-area term that means "can I borrow your lungs?")

During the construction phase of the facility, the big-money investors wanted some reassurance that the ALMA researchers would be working on solid, sober hard science. So the ALMA gang did what you or I would normally do to give investors confidence: they gathered up some locals and held a tribal ceremony that included a sacrificial "gratitude" offering to Pachamama.

~-~-~-~-~-~-~-~-~-~-~

Sidebar: World Cultures

Pachamama is the ancient Andean word for "Mother Nature." It's also the funniest name I've heard since "Andrew Weiner."

~-~-~-~-~-~-~-~-~-~-~

Sidebar: High Altitude Humor

Ancient Andean Retort: Dude, you smell like a rutting taruca.
Ancient Andean Comeback: So's your pachamama.

~-~-~-~-~-~-~-~-~-~-~

Anyway, the large, liberal-filmmaker-shaped object that ALMA just discovered is positioned somewhere between here and Alpha Centauri, the star system nearest to Earth except for *American Idol.* (Alpha Centauri also goes by the monikers a Cen, Rigil Kent, and Toliman, making it not only the nearest star system, but the first one to have aliases and, probably, a long rap sheet.)

Team ALMA are still arguing over whether this newly observed object is a planet, a star, or a spontaneously formed government bureaucracy. Part of the confusion is *because* it's never been noticed before, much like Lincoln Chafee's presidential campaign. Based on infrared signatures, Earth telescopes typically notice most large objects such as stars, planets, and Bill O'Reilly's ego. But this new "super-Earth" has eluded detection, leading sky-watchers to, well, guess (see *government bureaucracy*). And since we haven't had an acronym in here for nearly eight seconds, let's introduce Astronomical Units (AUs).

Astronomical Units were created by a Swedish scientist (Elmer Astronomical) to help measure vast numbers (see *current United States debt*). One AU is roughly the distance from the Earth to the Sun (E2S), or half the distance to the next freeway exit when you have pending bladder issues (PBI). One school of thought is that ALMA's new Super-Earth is 100 AUs from the Sun, which puts it farther out than the minor planet Sedna, a place so remote that it only has twelve McDonalds. Sedna, at 86 AUs, has a year that lasts 11,400 Earth years, so you can imagine how nasty their re-gifted Christmas fruitcakes are.

My favorite theory is that Earth Two is a "cool brown dwarf," like a young George Hamilton, or Tom Cruise in August. But I really think we all need to wait for some more hard scientific research, or at least another Pachamama sacrifice. After all, the website that announced the discovery of Earth Redux also offered links to other solid academic discussions, like "Hollywood's 15 Shortest Actresses" and "How Older Men Tighten Their Skin."

Although, you gotta admit – if it turns out there *are* two Earths, it's gonna be great fun watching Geraldo trying to out-ego himself...

Dead Again

When Acronyms Roamed the Earth

Folks, I'm afraid I have some bad news. Mankind is barreling along towards certain extinction.

Again.

Actually, this will be the sixth extinction. The *sixth*. Earth, it seems, is too stubborn to stay dead. Maybe *that's* what's behind our recent fascination with zombies.

And it's been a while since we had one -- dinosaurs were the fifth extinction. (You remember dinosaurs – those great big lizards who all died one Thursday because when they went outside to smoke they got hit by a giant meteor, starring Bruce Willis.) Extinction Five. That was, what, 65 million years ago? So, according to *Science Advances,* a not-well-known-and-for-a-reason journal that caters to the slide rule set, we're overdue.

That last wipe-out, the one that knocked off all the dinosaurs except Orrin Hatch, is known to people who have pocket protectors and wear elbow patches as the K-T extinction. And it's known as the K-T extinction despite the in-your-face fact that it occurred during the Cretaceous-Tertiary period, so why it's called the *K-T* instead of the *C-T* is beyond me. Maybe these scientists are smart, but they seem to have slept in at college and missed Acronym Day.

If you're like me, you probably never thought much about what was happening *before* dinosaurs ruled the Earth, back in the dark ages when we only had two genders. So, for the record, here are the first four extinctions:

- The Triassic-Jurassic: most of the planet's inhabitants died in a theater stampede at the premier of another Spielberg/Lucas prequel, *Jurassic Ball Park: The Umpire Strikes Back.*
- The Permian-Triassic: all life on Earth ended during World War Zero, which began after a really bad diplomatic blunder by John Kerry's ancestor, Ogg Kerry.
- The late Devonian: everything died due to either a massive drop in temperature or a massive rise in volcanic eruptions. Either it got too hot or it got too cold. We think. (I can't wait for the lame acronym on *this* one...)
- The Rollingstonian: during this first extinction, some 444 million years ago, everybody got wiped out, except Keith Richards.

Now keep in mind that all these multi-millennial "facts" are coming from a gaggle who can't even handle acronyms; heck, they'd probably name that giant phone company AT&. As a benchmark of their collective competence, here's a quote from a member of the 4-billion-year-old Earth school of experts:

"Many unsolved mysteries remain regarding these disasters, perhaps the greatest of which is what caused each of them."

Whew.

Again, that's an actual quote made with a straight face by a grownup. On the other hand, the "expert" was being quoted by NBC News, which is an oxymoron.

So, back here in the present, we're being warned that Extinction Six will be along shortly, putting all life on Earth at risk, except for cockroaches and Twinkies. And Keith Richards.

One of the main stormcrows in this latest round of doom-mongering is The World Wide Fund for Nature. By the way, the Word Wide Fund for Nature's acronym is *WWF*, not *WWFN*, as one might reasonably expect. Seriously. They blithely toss around half-baked acronyms like that, but yet they expect us to listen to their science. Phh.

The WWF claims that eighty kinds of freshwater fish have become extinct in the last 100 years, and that's not counting fish sticks, which during my own childhood were a seriously endangered species whenever they showed up at supper. And fifty of those eighty ex-fish families lived in and around (well, in) Africa's Lake Victoria and – if you believe the WWF version – vanished due to the introduction of some thug known as the voracious Nile perch. (acronym: N)

Dictionary Sidebar: *voracious* is a word that means "violently hungry," a term not often associated with Mrs. Paul's frozen foods.

Now, dictionary purists will point out that you *can't have* more than one extinction. By definition, if you're still around after an extinction, you're not extinct. But considering that we live in an epoch where "we 8 b4 u 2 lol" is a complete sentence, all rules are off.

But before you start running down 2 Rmageddons 'R' Us 4 post-extinction supplies, it should be noted that the website featuring the Six Extinctions piece also had an article with this dubious title:

Flying Bugs in Texas Show Up on Radar as Rainstorm

Imagine having your flight delayed because you were rerouted around a stationary front of ... moths.

Oh, and this one:

Patrick Stewart Backs Drones That Collect Whale Mucus

Actually, the on-staff scientists didn't use the term "mucus." They went with a more pedestrian word. A word that rhymes with *spot*. (Acronym: YUK)

First, Kirk, and now Picard. I don't know what it is about starship captains and whales. Somebody at the WWF should look into that.

But they better hurry.

Barry Parham

Stalking the Feral Chicken Salad
Airports and other alternate universes

I went to the airport twice this month, to remind myself why I hate going to the airport, and to gloat.

"Gloat? Why gloat?" you ask, assuming you're the type of person who lobs questions at inanimate objects, like humor columns, or that female glacier who's always in front of me at the grocery. I gloated because I wasn't flying *anywhere*, on *anything*, seated between *anybody* with Scotch breath and bladder issues. But this month I went to the airport to see some family off and to see them return, so I kept the gloating subdued; I don't think I actually broke out in audible song more than twice.

Flying is an activity that's solidly situated in my expanding List Of Things I Don't Like So Much, right in there between bear maulings, Al Gore doing stand-up comedy, and having my ears removed through my nose. The misery gauntlet known as "commercial airline travel" manages to combine many of my least favorite activities:

- negotiating with the No-Parking Nazis
- having strange people demand that I take off any of my clothes for free
- getting gang-groped by obese federal employees
- watching the inevitable clown imitating a running-late OJ Simpson leaping over luggage
- buying an indifferent chicken salad sandwich that was slapped together sometime during the Nixon administration and that's so overpriced you need a co-signer

What is it with the airport menu prices? Eight bucks for a hot dog. Yeah, that's fair. Chicken salad sandwich, $14.95. Is chicken salad that hard to catch? Is this some elusive Himalayan Yeti chicken that attacks without warning? Was the chicken armed?

Maybe I could just *rent* a sandwich.

And given the 50,000-percent markup prices attached to the food *outside* the plane, you'd think once you're *inside* the plane, the airline could afford to let us at more than three peanuts a pop. (The next time you start to get all bitter about your daily grind, remember that somewhere on this planet is a guy whose job is to make sure those little silver bags contain exactly three nuts.)

Another unexplained mystery about airports is that "please arrive early" game. If you're flying somewhere on, say, the tenth of June at 2.20pm, the airline wants you at the airport well ahead of 2.20pm, like March.

Winding Down Civilization

And having to show up at the airport early is doubly insulting because "departure time" has nothing whatsoever to do with the time the plane will actually take off. There hasn't been a plane that left a U.S. airport on time since the Enola Gay.

Of course, whenever airports are involved, there's also the statistically unavoidable potential for death (although it will be delayed). Death could occur if your plane crashes, or if you ate Nixon's chicken salad. Yeah, yeah, yeah, I know: it's usually right about here that the airline's PR department trots out some svelte beaming flunky, and she'll trill the memorized "don't worry" speech about how you're so much more likely to be in an accident in a car than in a plane. Yeah, yeah, yeah. All I know is the chances of me falling 20,000 feet out of my car at 500 miles per hour are really, really slim.

Though sometimes I do run out of peanuts.

Even if you do eventually get where you're going, you may find that your luggage had other plans. In 2004, over 17,000 claims of baggage theft were reported. When I travel in my car, I almost *never* have to worry about suitcases vanishing, unless I'm in Detroit.

In that same year, sixty baggage screeners were arrested for baggage theft; in other words, the people getting paid to make sure the luggage you brought was safe were BUSY making sure it wasn't safe for you to bring any luggage. By 2008, the number of baggage thefts had more than doubled, which is what the Obama administration calls a "positive employment trend."

And the trend continues. As of 2011, the TSA employed about 60,000 screeners, and at least 500 of those stellar public servants have been fired or suspended for stealing stuff from your luggage. This is what TSA watchdogs call a "procedural glitch," or as we would put it, "felony theft."

The TSA blames this "non-optimal trend" on poor morale. Maybe they should hold some morale-boosting seminars ... you know, taxpayer-funded hotel weekends, free entertainment, open bar, catered meals.

I know where they can get some top-notch chicken salad.

DWI (Dating While Inhaling)

I love you...what was your name again?

<><><>~~~~~~~~~~~~~~~~~~~~~~~~~<><><>

Well, the numbers are in! And it looks like online dating not only works; it's become wildly popular...even among married people. So now, it's inevitable that our selfie-self-obsessed society move on to the next fad: online divorcing.

But until somebody comes up with *that* website, it's worth nothing that online dating has started to move into niche marketing – very specialized partner matching for partner shoppers with specific partner desires. You've seen, around the web, some of these narrowly focused "X looking for Y" postings...

- Middle-aged Packers fan looking for fun-loving single lady in Green Bay who likes football.
- Native American professor of economics seeks mute woman to share weekend water sports.
- Unemployed pole dancer seeks bed-ridden octogenarian with massive investment income. Please send picture of wallet.

- Single vegetarian looking for one or more females named Amber to share my love of curd. Faint odor of patchouli a plus.
- Slowly aging non-denominational Eastern European vampire with great hair looking to meet six or seven Rubenesque brunettes for candlelit dinners, carriage rides, and shape-shifting. Involves some physical discomfort and occasional dying.

One such niche website is aimed at pot smokers who can't seem to find a date, possibly because they dozed out before leaving for the singles bar. The site and its members refer to themselves as The Cupids of Cannabis. Apparently, somebody had already snatched up "The Bong & the Restless." (their motto: "all doped up and nowhere to go")

If you visit the doped daters website, you'll first be required to fill out their signup form; you know, because they want to screen out any irresponsible losers from the legitimate losers. After all, you don't want to waste your time with reckless rabble, if you're discerning enough to scour the internet looking for lonely people with illegal substance issues.

Well of *course* I filled out the form.

It's a fairly standard signup form...with a few novel touches. Next to each data entry box is a helpful little "What it this?" popup. Hover over the What Does This Mean icon and you get a short description of what you're supposed to enter in that box, in case this is your first visit to this planet, or you're already stoned.

First, you're asked to pick your "Profile Type." The Profile Type dropdown list options are "Single," or "Couple," which seems a bit unfair to pipe-huffing polygamists, but I'm here to report, not to judge.

If you hover over the profile type's What Does This Mean, you'll get this handy advice: Select "Couple" if you are joining as a couple (see *already stoned*)

Next on the form is *Sex* (the gender, not the contact sport), followed by *Looking For*. Both option's options are limited to Man and Woman. Interestingly, however, *Sex* is a radio button, meaning you can only select one, but *Looking For* is a set of checkboxes, meaning you can select one, or the other, or both. So at The Cupids of Cannabis, you're allowed to *look for* a man and a woman, but you're not allowed to *be* a man and a woman. That's bad news for the gender-straddlers out there: Bruce Jenner; Dennis Rodman; the person who picks out Hillary's clothes.

The signup form concludes with the standard stuff – name, username, password, the little checkbox ratifying that you agree to the terms blah blah and agree not to blah blah or to sue anybody over blah blah. One more thing...What Does This Mean is also there to guide you through the tricky shoals of typing your own name: next to First Name, the handy tip "Enter your first name" and next to...yeah, you guessed it..."Enter your last name."

Obviously, the clientele at Cupids are *seriously* high.

Once you've successfully joined – and paused to scarf down some munchies – you can get straight (no pun intended) to the task of finding somebody with a compatible water pipe, or you can take a minute to complete a Personality Profile.

According to the Cupids' personality test, there are sixteen personality types (I suppose if you're joining as a couple, there are only eight.) Of course, sixteen personality types is just silly non-science. Everybody knows there are only twelve types of people, and they're already being served at another dating website, The Hashish of Horoscopes.

Another especially targeted online resource caters to married people who still want to date (looks like *somebody* forgot to read the rules, *hmm?*) My favorite part about this website are the tips – staggeringly hypocritical advice on how to be the best on your block at destroying your marriage. Witness:

If you can't respect yourself, how are you going to be able to respect her?

That's so true. A real man shows respect for the woman he's using to cheat on his wife.

And here's another:

You don't have to have the rugged looks of James Dean or the wit and eloquence of James Bond; you just need to be personal, affable and honest.

That's right. When you're advertising for infidelity, it's important to be honest.

How To Hate Everybody, Just A Little

In a politically correct world, a mandate is just a date

<><><>~~~~~~~~~~~~~~~~~~~~~~~~<><><>

Microaggression. It's the latest rage, pun intended.

At some point while we were all distracted, probably by a text message, America's leaders, educators, and media morphed into a rabid cottage industry of culture groomers and ego protectors. It abruptly became the collective (and unsolicited) duty of these Uber-Nannies to proactively make sure nobody anywhere ever gets offended, insulted, sad, or disliked.

It's as if we'd suddenly become a giant kindergarten, but with taxes.

And now, in the latest attempt to make sure nobody is ever unhappy, North Carolina State University has published a helpful "microaggression tool" guideline.

Well, they certainly got the "tool" part right.

23

The tool was published by NC State ombuds, Roy Baroff. (See how absurd it gets? Once the politically correct dialogue Nazis get involved, you can't even say *ombudsman* anymore.)

Man...uh, I mean, uh, *Person*. This is getting out of control. We need some common sense. And we need to...uh...to de*person*d it, now.

NC State's tool (the document, or Roy, you decide) defines microaggressions as "everyday verbal or nonverbal slights, snubs, or insults, intentional or unintentional." Oh, good – at least the definition's not overly broad or anything. See, the problem is that microaggressions may "communicate hostile, derogatory, or negative messages" that, intentionally or not, might target people "based on their marginalized group membership." In other words, unless you're a clone surrounded by clones, just keep your mouth shut.

Now, according to the most recent dictionary I can trust (Webster's Unabridged,1983), aggression is defined as *an act of hostility*, or *an unprovoked attack*. In my Webster's, *microaggression* isn't even listed, which must really irritate any NC State coeds looking to file microaggression lawsuits...if we can still say *coed*.

So maybe my Webster's covers "microaggessions" by default...as "agressions." An aggression might be somebody dope-slapping an overly obnoxious ombuds, or it might be that unpleasant thing that seems to happen every time Alec Baldwin talks to a reporter.

(By the way, I favor my dictionary – the 1983 Webster's New Universal Unabridged Dictionary, Second Edition, which runs to some 2,129 pages, not counting maps and oversized attorney refrigerator magnets – because it is a sensible word authority that predates such recent non-English irritations like *LOL*, *my bad*, *selfie*, and using *interface* as a verb.)

I don't know if you're ready for this, but here are some ombuds-inspired examples of microaggression:

Your dress looks nice.
That's right. You can't just waltz about, spewing shallow sexist slurs like that anymore. Unless you're talking to a guy. *That* would be fine.

How's your wife?
The preferred non-microaggressive question would be "how's your spouse?" or "how's your significant other?" or "so, do you still beat your gender-transitioning life partner or, as the case may be, partners?"

I think the most qualified person should get the job.
Believe it or not, there's a hidden message here, according to the tool and the tool's tool: "Black people have an unfair advantage, and that's unfair to those of us being unfair to black people."
I know how to put this one to rest: have Michael Jackson compete with John Boehner for the same position, and let's see who gets the job – the peach guy or the orange guy.

Wanna go play some golf?
I can only quote the tool on this one: "This could be deemed offensive to someone who hasn't had the experience." I see. So if you weren't actually delivered at childbirth while clutching a

seven iron, you could be psychically scarred for life if someone invited you to spend a Saturday wearing plaid pants and drinking cheap beer. Okay, bad example.

So, where you from?
This one, I can barely believe. In fact, the entire Southern United States would collapse into a mute stupor if nobody's mother was allowed to ask you, "So, son, where do you go to church?"

Stupidity aside, my staff and I always want to be helpful, not to just point and laugh (oh, don't worry – we'll get to that later). So may we leave you with a much more useful list – a compilation of some seriously aggressive comments. *(source: The Miss Universe Omsbudwoman Pageant, brought to you by Donald Trump)*

Hope this helps.

Things I Bet You Better Not Say

- Wow, it's true. White people *can't* dance.
- So, when are you due?
- More rice? (or chicken, gumbo, pasta, potatoes, altar boys, booze, watermelon, haggis)
- Yo, Guido!
- I bet you're great at basketball. (or math, yoga, lying, guilt, farming, finance, avoiding taxes, selling pot, making haggis)
- You got a C in algebra? But you're Asian!
- You know, for a Jew, you don't sweat much.

Winding Down Civilization

- I love what you've done with your hairs.
- Did your parents have any children that lived?
- I'm impressed. Not all obese women can wear gauchos.
- Here's a thought – before you dress yourself, turn on the lights.
- Do you always smell like that?
- There's no way you can fit in that car. What, are you gonna get a running start?
- You know, a good doctor could fix that nose.
- Obama's *black?*

Barry Parham

Shabani & Cousin Bonobo

Hey, apes are people, too

<><><>~~~~~~~~~~~~~~~~~~~~~~~~~<><><>

It's been a wild week, what with escaped convicts, ISIS attacks, Supreme Court rulings, and of course, the bitter earth-shattering news that the host of *The Tonight Show* hurt his hand. But let's not waste any more time on trivialities – let's get to the real news.

There's a gorilla in a Japanese zoo that women think is hot.

Now, I know what you're thinking. Maybe we should give the womenfolk of Japan a break. Maybe the gorilla, comparatively speaking, is a looker. After all, these women live in a country where the top models of male perfection are suicide pilots, Pat Morita and Godzilla.

But apparently Japanese women are gaga over Shabani, an 18-year-old western lowland gorilla who lives in Higashiyama Zoo and Botanical Gardens in the city of Nagoya, which I think was the name of a general in one of the *Star Trek* movies. The ladies are flocking to the zoo to see Shabani's "handsome looks and dramatic poses" and they're tweeting things like "I

29

went to Higashiyama Zoo. This hot Shabani ikemen was certainly handsome." (*ikemen*, I'm told, translates roughly as "good-looking man." I have no idea how you say "gaga" in Japanese.)

And now that the U.S. Supreme Court has redefined the age-old covenant of marriage to be ... as Godzilla might put it ... *anata ga yaritaidesu* ("pretty much anything goes"), Shabani will be uploading his dating profile to Match.com.

In case Shabani turns out to be the humble type and doesn't fully open up in the online dating world, I'll share what little I've been able to learn about this hirsute hunk, this buff Japanese-chick-slaying father of two. The western gorilla, which some extremely non-creative taxonomists tagged as *Gorilla gorilla*, is sorted into two gorilla subspecies, and Shabani belongs to the western lowland gorilla gang (a gang classified with the lazy-bordering-on-insulting Latin moniker *Gorilla gorilla gorilla*). At that rate, then, I suppose Shabani's two kids will be stuck with *Gorilla gorilla gorilla gorilla*, which later in life will be really hard to fit on their business cards.

Although these gorillas hail from the Congo, Shabani was born in the Netherlands and raised in a zoo in Sydney, Australia, so he's definitely a man of the wor ... um ... primate of the world. That bon vivant worldliness could help explain the chick magnet's Japanese popularity; women love an ape that can tell a good story.

In the wild (literal translation: *Detroit*), *Gorilla gorilla gorilla* usually lives in a group consisting of one guy and five or six gorillettes, an arrangement known among humans as "polygamy," and to the U.S. Supreme Court as "next." Interestingly, the young male *Gorilla g. g.'s* will leave their natal group and go through a "bachelor" stage that can last for several years and will incorporate a great deal of sexual angst, take-out pizza, and bad barstool decisions. (This occurs before the ape achieves sexual maturity, which is an oxymoron if I ever heard one.)

Conversely, *Gorilla gorilla gorilla* females in the wild are never found alone, especially when they're in a restaurant and one needs to go to the ladies' room. The distaff *G. g. g.* just travel from breeding group to breeding group, like some college sororities, or Paris Hilton.

Biologists note that the western lowland gorilla exhibits pronounced sexual dimorphism, which isn't nearly as dirty as it sounds. It turns out that that fifty-dollar phrase basically means the guys are bigger than the girls. A world-shaking scientific observation like that ranks right up there on the "I Did Not Need To Be Told That-o-meter" with this one:

The brains of many mammals, including humans, are significantly different for males and females of the species.

Wow. Men and women are different. Who knew?

It's interesting to note that *Gorilla cubed* shares the Congo with another ape of some importance, if you believe in the theory of evolution (and if you've ever met a network television programming executive, you do). According to some seriously dull science writers, the bonobo is a very close relative – the closest cousin, some say – of *Homo sapiens* (that's all of us, except for Dennis Rodman).

The bonobo is a type of chimpanzee, one of the endangered "great apes" that, like Shabani, inhabit the Congo Basin in central Africa. Long ago, people used to refer to the bonobo as a "pygmy" or "dwarf" chimpanzee, but then somebody discovered political correctness and a discrimination lawsuit was filed by the ACLU (African Chimpanzee Lawyers Union).

But what's most interesting about Cousin Bonobo -- especially in light of the Supreme Court's recent redefining of marriage as something somewhere between an *a la carte* menu and an all-you-can-eat buffet -- is that the chimp is one of several animals that exhibit homosexual behavior. And for a sheltered little rube like me, I found that list surprisingly diverse.

(By the way, the term *homosexual* was coined in 1868 by an Austrian named Karl-Maria Kertbeny, possibly because his name was Karl-Maria. K-M is also famous for being the first child in schoolyard games during recess to be both Shirts *and* Skins.)

Anyway, here's a partial list of gay animals (source: the official voter registration committee for the "Hillary Clinton 2016" campaign):

- Giraffes ("come on up and see me sometime")
- Bison (that'll leave a mark)
- Dolphins (oh...so "Flipper" was a *verb*)
- Vultures (the birds, not the politicians)

- Penguins (but they never know it, 'cause they all look alike anyway)
- Elephants (so *that's* what they never forget)
- Sheep (don't even go there)
- Dragonflies (who's doing this research?)
- Bonobos and other apes

Uh oh. Bonobos *and other apes?*

Imagine the crushed reaction in Japanese ladies' rooms if Shabani's gay!

Barry Parham

A Boy Renamed Sue

Crackers. Crayons. Cross-dressing.

<>< ><>~~~~~~~~~~~~~~~~~~~~~~~~<><><>

Remember the good old days, when children had childhoods? Well, I hope you took plenty of pictures, 'cause childhood just got cancelled.

Yes, America. Thanks to the gentle guidance of President Barack "Congress, Shmongress" Obama and the Federal Gender Identity Police, your elementary school children will soon be sharing the same bathroom, regardless of hateful, bigoted, outdated biology concepts like "girls" and "boys."

Apparently, lots of concerned people in the nation's capital are under the impression that first- and second-graders all across America can't empty their bladders at school, due to deep anxieties about "gender identification." And the little tykes are psychically frustrated because they're "forced" to use gender-specific restroom facilities.

Keep in mind ... these are kids who only recently acquired the skills necessary to successfully break a graham cracker in half.

You might be thinking that elementary school is a little early to be bothering small children with "mature" social topics like sexual orientation, gender reassignments, and why Hillary Clinton sounds like the illegitimate love child of Selma Diamond and Louis Armstrong. But that's just because you're a hateful bigot.

Small children are obviously ready to grasp life-altering decisions like gender identification. And then, nap time.

~-~-~-~-~-~-~-~-~-~-~-~

Federal Nanny: Hi, young man!

Small Child: Hi.

Fed: I'm sorry...you don't mind if I refer to you as a *male*, do you?

Child: Huh?

Fed: Or as *young*?

Child: Huh?

Fed: What's your name?

Child: Timmy.

Fed: How old are you, Timmy?

Child: Seven.

Fed: And what do *you* identify as?

Child: Timmy.

~-~-~-~-~-~-~-~-~-~-~-~

Clearly, Timmy needs therapy.

Later that morning...

~-~-~-~-~-~-~-~-~-~-~-~

Timmy: Sally, what are you *doing* in here? This is the *little boys'* room!

Sally: Not any more. The President of the United States says I can utilize any public bathroom that validates my personal gender identity choices.

Timmy: Wow-wee, that's a lotta big words for a second-grader.

Sally: I also identify as a twenty-eight-year-old Wharton graduate.

Timmy: What's a worten?

Sally: So. This is what the boys' room looks like. Gross.

Timmy: Actually, guys don't really talk all that much in here.

~-~-~-~-~-~-~-~-~-~-~-~

Let's hope Timmy remembers to wash up! Because soon he'll be in the cafeteria, throwing away his government-mandated lunch!

And later that evening...

~-~-~-~-~-~-~-~-~-~-~

Mom: Timmy, do you have any homework?

Timmy: I'm not sure.

Mom: What's *that* supposed to mean?

Timmy: Well, the teacher said we should embrace gender assignment. Is that like a reading assignment?

~-~-~-~-~-~-~-~-~-~-~

So where does it end? If a guy identifies as a woman, does he deserve discount shooters on Ladies Night? Does he suddenly start acquiring shoes?

If a woman identifies as a man, does she suddenly start watching reruns of *Baywatch*? Will she suddenly start making "pull my finger" jokes? Or start carrying a ridiculous number of grocery bags from the car to the kitchen to avoid making more than one trip? Will she suddenly think the Three Stooges are hilarious?

If Bill Clinton identifies as a female, would he then hit on himself? If Bruce Jenner started calling himself Gypsy Rose Lee, would he get paid to pose in a swimsuit? Okay, bad example.

Can Gloria Estefan identify as a rich fat white man and join that exclusive country club? Can I identify as a Native

American and open a casino and sell cigarettes? Can Dennis Rodman identify as a bride? Okay, bad example.

Sometime in the near future, at an office park downtown...

~.~.~.~.~.~.~.~.~.~.~.~

Desk Jockey: Hi. Welcome to the Small Business Administration. How can I help you, sir?

Bob: Ma'am.

DJ: Sorry.

Bob: Anybody ever tell you you're cute?

DJ: Stop that.

Bob: I'd like to apply for your Startup Business Loan for Female Entrepreneurs program.

DJ: But you're not a woman.

Bob: Yes, I am.

DJ: Obviously, you're a guy. I'm a guy, too. I know a guy when I see one. Plus, you're wearing a work shirt with the name "Bob" stenciled on the pocket.

Bob: I'm identifying as a woman. Have been, since about eight-thirty.

DJ: Oh. Okay. Sign here.

Bob: I'm also black.

DJ: Okay, sign here, too.

Bob: And Chinese.

DJ: You're gonna need some help carrying all this cash out to your car.

Bob: And Jewish.

DJ: I got nothing.

Bob: I meant Muslim.

DJ: Ah. Sign here.

Bob: So, what're you doing later, big boy?

DJ: Please stop that.

~-~-~-~-~-~-~-~-~-~-~-~

The Third Oldest Profession

Unreality TV at its finest

<><><>~~~~~~~~~~~~~~~~~~~~~~~~~<><><>

Good evening, everybody. I'm Duff Holstein, and welcome to tonight's first Presidential primary debate, brought to you by American's top cable news channel, A Bunch of Fair & Balanced Hot Women News.

Tonight, we're coming to you live, direct from the Quicken Loans Arena in beautiful downtown Cleveland. Okay, downtown Cleveland. We are more or less glad to be here, just scant feet away from the Cuyahoga River, a river that once actually caught on fire. So here's your first debate tip of the evening: *bottled water.*

With me tonight to help moderate the inaugural debate are two of my esteemed colleagues from A Bunch of Fair & Balanced Hot Women News. I know you'll all recognize Sage Jowls, who's been covering the Washington DC beat since Nixon bought his first Walkman. And on my right is Jennifer Lithe, a smokin' hot geopolitical expert who has practically zero body fat and who once spelled the word *inaugural* correctly, allegedly.

41

Our audience analysis experts over in Marketing are predicting that some 24 million people will be tuning in to watch tonight's Presidential primary debate, which coincidentally is the same number of people that are *running* for President. The 2016 slate even includes one seriously persistent guy named Jack Fellure who's officially been pursuing the White House top job in every election since 1988. Heck, nobody's worked that hard to get in to the Oval Office since Monica.

And speaking of Monica, sources have hinted that one person who will *not* be watching tonight's debate is the Democrat candidate for President, Hillary "The People's Uterus" Clinton. (Later that night, as it turns out, The Shrill showcased her vast qualifications to be leader of the free world by taking a selfie with Kim Kardashian.)

Obviously we would never intentionally jam several million politicians into an oversized basketball court, not even in Cleveland. So here's what we decided to do: we picked the top ten candidates, based on an average of the most recent polls, even if the polls suggested some unbelievably absurd trend, like, say, Donald Trump leading the pack. Those ten candidates will line up for their debate at 9pm, while the next seven poll favorites will convene a few hours earlier, at 5pm, when everybody in America is not watching because they're driving home from work.

Now, as the dictionary tells us, a *debate* is classically defined as "a formal discussion in which opposing arguments are put forward." But here at A Bunch of Fair & Balanced Hot Women News, we take a broader approach to the term, which basically means there'll be pretty much zero actual debating going on, while we focus instead on hoping some candidate will blow up and say something so blindingly stupid that it will ruin their reputation forever.

Here are the rules. Prior to all the "debating," the candidates will all walk in, stand at the front of the stage and smile, except for Donald Trump, who always looks like he just bit into a bad oyster. The candidates will then wave at various people in the audience, while occasionally pointing with a conspiratorial wink, or feigning pleased surprise that *that* guy showed up, in that offhand way that political types seem to instinctively know from birth.

The moderators will ask each candidate ridiculously broad, complex questions, and the candidate will then have seven seconds to reply. A "ding" tone will sound if they talk too long. The tone sounds like this:

ding

Each Republican candidate has pledged to abide by tonight's format. And each candidate has pledged not to hug Barack Obama in the aftermath of coastal flooding in New Jersey, unless it's an election year.

After the debate has ended, we'll have another round of waving, followed by the inevitable whining from some candidate carping about being ignored by the moderator.

And now, let's meet the candidates. For tonight's prime time debate, here are the ten top-tier contestants, arranged by height, tiniest to tallest:

- Rand Paul
- Mike Huckabee
- Marco Rubio
- Chris Christie
- John Kasich
- Ben Carson
- Ted Cruz
- Donald Trump (without his hair, he'd be next to Mike)
- Scott Walker
- Jeb Bush

And for the 5pm rush hour debate, here are the next seven most-favorite candidates, arranged in order of successful hits by facial recognition software:

- Rick Perry
- Carly Fiorina
- Bobby Jindal
- Rick Santorum
- George Pataki
- Lindsey Graham
- Jim Something or Other

Okay, let's get to debating! We'll begin with this first question, for Donald Trump.

Rand Paul: Hey, what about me?

Ted Cruz: Hello? What am I, invisible?

Holstein: Mr. The Donald, as President of the United States, what will you do on your first day in office?

Donald Trump: First, I would outlaw ObamaCare and Rosie O'Donnell. No, wait. Rosie first, then ObamaCare. Next, I wou...

ding

Barry Parham

Life'll Kill Ya

Dangers. Hazards. Tropical fruit.

<><><>~~~~~~~~~~~~~~~~~~~~~~~~~<><><>

Yeah, I know, I know. Warren Zevon said it first.

In fact, *Life'll Kill Ya* was the title (and the title track) of his tenth album. I remember. This was back in the good old days, when musicians still used actual music in their music, instead of just a lot of loops and yelling. Oh, bands still got angry back then, but they remembered to use chords, too.

But Warren was right: life'll kill ya. And, in fact, the "Excitable Boy" – the man who gave us *Werewolves of London* -- checked out over a decade ago. He had all of Keith Richard's habits, but none of his luck.

Life'll kill ya, all right. And it'll sneak right up on ya, too. For example, here are some unexpected things that can kill ya, things you never imagined might be heading your way:

- The American government has decided the best way to keep Iran from getting nuclear weapons is to give Iran nuclear weapons.

- Last year, five people died from getting attacked by a shark (*source: Stephen Spielberg's horrifying movie, "Jaws"*). But 150 people died from getting hit on the head by a coconut. (*source: Stephen Spielberg's next horrifying movie, "Husk"*)

- Despite decades of narcissism-induced nausea, Geraldo Rivera is still allowed on TV.

- In the United States, 450 people die every year from falling out of bed. If coconuts every start sleeping in beds, we'll have to call in the National Guard.

- At one point during our early tactical maneuvers against ISIS, the Secretary of State deployed ... I am not good enough to make this stuff up ... James Taylor. And they didn't even arm him with a proper microphone. I wouldn't have been a bit surprised if the legendary singer had busted out in an all-new, Pentagon-commissioned tune, "Carpet-Shower the People."

- Aliens from outer space are monitoring a volcano under Yellowstone National Park. (*source: Geraldo Rivera*)

- We're about to pick a President, and our choices are an alleged conservative that women can't stand, or an alleged woman that *nobody* can stand.

- Aliens are also monitoring the Presidential elections. They're leaning toward Bernie.

- There are no States left that will accept ObamaCare. But you still have to buy it.

- A woman has OD'd on Johnson & Johnson's Baby Powder.

- No, seriously.

That's right. Now, even baby powder can kill you, unless you're Keith Richards. Baby powder! When I was growing up, the only thing in our house more common than baby powder was fish sticks. Baby powder, deadly? That's like saying peanut butter & jelly sandwiches are fatal. Or layaway.

Earlier this year, a judge ordered Johnson & Johnson to cough up *seventy-two million dollars* in an anti-baby powder decision, according to the internet, an infallible source of knowledge since Al Gore invented it during the Punic Wars. It seems that the accusing lawyers were able to prove to a jury that a Missouri woman's demise was due to decades of exposure to talcum powder (well, what did you *think* "baby" powder was made of, babies? We're talking about Johnson & Johnson here, not Planned Parenthood.) So the prosecution made its case, the judge ruled in favor of the woman's family, and J&J wrote a post-dated check for $72 million. (After attorney fees, the family took home $23.50)

As it turns out, there are currently several hundred lawsuits plaguing the dual Johnsons, makers of such common household products as Tylenol, Listerine, Bengay, Visine, and Band-Aids. (Band-Aids were added as an afterthought, once all the other bathroom products started exploding.)

Basically, the accusations are that Johnson Squared has known for decades that talcum powder will mess you up quicker than a sleepwalking coconut. In particular, baby powder seems to be linked to Ovarian Cancer, which is either a medical condition or the name of an extra from *Julius Caesar*. To back up this claim, a doctor from Harvard testified that talc is "probably" a contributing factor in about 10,000 cases of ovarian cancer each year, after which the physician witness "probably" got paid.

This news led Bruce Jenner to file his-or-her own lawsuit, since he-or-she identifies as an ovarian cancer survivor, despite the fact that Mr. or Mrs. Jenner doesn't even *have* any ovarians.

Personally, I don't know if talc will kill you or not. But if we're going to start banning stuff, I vote for outlawing another evil from my childhood: Mercurochrome. That is one seriously sadistic product, and given my childhood clumsiness, I *stayed* soaked in Mercurochrome. I don't know what's in that nasty little bottle, but it burns like the drool from one of Ridley Scott's aliens.

Especially when you get up at night and bark your shin on a coconut.

Shrimp Knuckles

WARNING: this article may contain Nobel Prize spoilers

<><><>~~~~~~~~~~~~~~~~~~~~~~~~~~~~~<><><>

Everybody loves a scientist. They create stuff we depend on, they generally pose no threat of stealing your girlfriend, and those function-first corduroy pants they wear make funny noises when they walk.

Scientists are a unique breed, with peculiar habits:

- They love to sort stuff. (I once dated somebody who sorted my books by height. I forget her name now...in fact, I forgot her name *then* -- immediately, somewhere between C and D.)
- They insist on measuring things, and then they insist on measuring them again. (no, I will *not* be discussing *that* date)
- Not only can scientists pronounce 47-syllable chemical compounds, names of rare diseases, and all the carcinogens lurking in a buttered bagel, but they seem to genuinely enjoy doing it. (This makes scientists extremely popular as "expert witnesses" in product

51

liability lawsuits, which in and of itself can be a lucrative career option.)

The best-known scientists *become* best-known by focusing on a specific scientific discipline, or by irritating the Spanish Inquisition. For example, we remember Galileo as the "father of modern astronomy" and the "father of physics." (back home in Pisa, he was also known as the "father of three illegitimate kids," but let's not drag the Inquisition back into it)

Other famous scientific specialists who've made their mark on mankind include:

- Thales of Miletus, top sage among the original Seven Sages of Athens, who invented the *hypothesis*, which is why he's known as the "father of ridiculously overpaid corporate consultants"
- Aristotle, the 2,300-year-old Greek thinker whose seminal hip-hop rocker, *Aristotelian Epistemology*, was the first album to be reviewed by Dick Clark
- Leonardo da Vinci, who, in an effort to get rid of a clinging groupie named Mona Lisa, invented the helicopter
- Gregor Mendel, the co-inventor of jeans (along with Levi Strauss, who gave us the waltz)
- Jonas Salk, who discovered a cure for Poland

More recently, we can point to Max Planck, who created quantum theory in order to calculate the probability that he could get that weird "c" removed from his last name. For his efforts, Max initially received the 1918 Nobel Prize in Physics, but it was recalled and given to Barack Obama, whom the mainstream media also credited with winning the 1918 World Series and curing the Great Flu Pandemic. And let's not forget Albert Einstein, who invented *gravitas*, the universal constant defining "dignity in leadership," except in Congress.

Throughout history, scientists have thought long and hard before selecting the field of scientific study to which they will dedicate their corduroyed lives. Some have chosen to chase the cure for a disease; others have dedicated their lives to agriculture, or horticulture, or to chasing a cure for the Culture Club. To be sure, a few have simply sold out for easy buckets of government grant money, and then spent their professional lives putting shrimp on treadmills, and measuring the shrimp's stress, and I am not good enough to make this stuff up.

But now we hear from a scientist, holed up in the University of Alberta, who has hitched his claim-to-fame wagon to a seriously narrow niche: his goal is to unlock an age-old scientific enigma, one that has plagued humanity since the dawn of time: When you crack your knuckles, what's that popping noise?

Yes, the bold, trail-blazing pioneers at U of A are careening toward Nobel history with their ground-breaking look inside...finger joints. To collect their measurements, they nominated one member of the team (probably by secret ballot), laid him face-down on a table, and then inserted his fingers, one at a time, into a tube connected to a cable that was slowly pulled until the knuckle popped.

I can hear the speaker in Stockholm now...

"For their innovative work in the crowded but crucial field of "Pull My Finger" jokes, this year's Nobel Prize goes to..."

The conclusion from Alberta? That popping noise when you crack your knuckles is due to the rapid creation of a gas-filled cavity, which, coincidentally, is how members of Congress are made.

Of course, since I was on the internet, the online knuckle story offered clicks to an article about men who film shrimp in slow-motion, a fight between liquid mercury and corn syrup, and an 11-minute YouTube video of the World's Roundest Objects.

But let's not drag Congress back into it.

See EU Later

All rose as the Queen made her brentrance...

<><><>~~~~~~~~~~~~~~~~~~~~~~~~~~<><><>

This past week has been an interesting one, for those of us in America who are fascinated by all things British, or invasive dental surgery. Here's a quick headline recap:

- The United Kingdom voted to leave the European Union
- In Texas, England invaded a Mexican woman's mouth

You can't have missed these stories in the news, unless you don't read, in which case we have to wonder why you're sitting there staring vacantly at a humor column. But that's entirely your business; besides, being brand-dead isn't necessarily a dead end...just because a person is terminally clueless doesn't mean they can't pursue a successful career in politics.

The first story is the one getting the lion's share of news coverage, mostly because, unlike the second story, it's true. Last week, the citizens of the United Kingdom – a tenuous alliance that includes England, Scotland, Ireland, Wales, and

Orlando – voted to pull out of the European Union, which is in Europe, for those of you pursuing a career in politics.

There were several reasons driving England's decision, including high taxes and repressive regulation imposed by an external governing authority...an irony not lost on students of the American Revolution. However, some more level-headed analysts think Britain simply got tired of taking orders from a country responsible for inventing Brussels sprouts.

Okay, that's not entirely fair. Over the centuries, continental Europe has made several important contributions to world culture, including the Spanish Inquisition, the continental breakfast, and the plague...though we're not all that impressed with the breakfast.

To be sure, British cuisine is notoriously not cuisine, either. But they do know how to lay on a good breakfast, even if they insist on calling bacon "rashers." Brits also carelessly toss around words like plebiscite, battlebus, and bangers and mash, as if they'd invented the English language or something.

The other story in the news involves the English language, too, so let's get to it. This was a story that started out really interesting and sped straight to silly. According to the report, there's a woman of Mexican heritage living in Texas – I know, hard to swallow – and she underwent some kind of jaw surgery. After the surgery, according to her, she suddenly, involuntarily, began speaking with a ridiculously bad British accent, as if she were channeling Keanu Reeves in *Dracula*.

"I didn't notice it at first," she claimed, "but my husband told me I was talking funny." In fact, a Houston pathologist diagnosed her with Foreign Accent Syndrome, an extremely rare condition that hasn't been documented since Dick Van Dyke starred in *Mary Poppins*. And the recuperating Hispanic might have gotten away with it, too, except she suddenly started using words like *blimey* and went around calling people *blokes* and *gov'nor*. And though the medical community may agree that a head injury can cause changes in speech patterns, no known malady can make somebody grow a thesaurus. Now, she's been debunked as self-serving and dishonest, and will have to spend the rest of her life pursuing a career in politics.

Anyway, back to Britain. After nearly twenty-five years of being ordered around by unelected bureaucrats in another country, the citizens of England have decided to return to what they'd been doing for the last thousand years: being ordered around by unelected bureaucrats at home.

Some over-caffeinated liberal-minded news analysts see Britain's anti-EU move as racism; some see it as class warfare. This is nonsense, of course: I mean, it's not like England has an actual queen living in an actual castle or anything. But the history of British government is filled with unique details like that: for example, their Speaker of the House is not allowed to speak, and if you've ever seen Nancy Pelosi, you'd have to admire their thinking.

Of course, the media have coined a cute, catchy term for the British withdrawal from the EU: they've dubbed it the *brexit*. (BR-itish EXIT. Get it? See what they did there?) And now that England has set the self-rule precedent, at least five other

European nations have announced possible plans to follow England's lead, all except for that part about driving on the wrong side of the road.

Unfortunately, as more EU member nations consider jumping ship, we'll be inundated by more bilge from the various news outlets' Departments of Cute & Catchy. After all, why stop with Brexit?

- Germany: Grexit
- Departugal
- Nowayout
- Latervia
- Finish
- Italeave
- Czechout
- Byegium

Blimey.

Michael Phelps para o Presidente
...featuring The Large, Hairy Girl From Ipanema

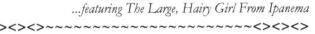

It happens every four years. I don't know if it's a coincidence, or some cruel cosmic prank, but every four years we've somehow ended up with two great big, loud, overwhelming events occurring in the same year: the Olympic Games and a Presidential election. One is an honest, honorable gathering of a country's most worthy competitors. Guess which.

I don't know. Maybe it's some kind of galactic punishment, some interplanetary payback for inventing reality TV.

This year, Rio de Janeiro was selected as the host city for the Olympic Games, largely due to their world-class poverty, political corruption, soaring crime rate, and large quantities of raw sewage. It's like Detroit, but with a beach.

According to NBC News, which gives you some idea of the amount of time I spent researching this column, there are rivers in Rio that contain *seventeen million* times the acceptable amount of water pollution permitted by our federal government here at home, except for rivers in Colorado that the EPA personally poisons. One NBC reporter covering beach volleyball even claimed to have seen body parts washing ashore during a practice round. (Authorities quickly determined the limbs belonged to a Bernie Sanders staffer who was preparing to testify against the Clinton Foundation, but NBC didn't mention that.)

Also, one of the Olympic swimming contestants complained that the water in the practice pool tasted soapy, but after talking to the volleyball team, he quit whining.

The games hadn't even begun yet, when we heard that three Olympic athletes and one Russian diplomat had already been mugged (see *slow news day in Detroit*). Actually, the Russian fought back, shooting and killing his assailant. The diplomat received a score of 8.5 from the Olympic judges and a pardon from Bill Clinton.

Speaking of Russia, there are 118 overzealous Russian athletes who won't be competing at all in Rio; they were banned after getting caught doping up with steroids, various farm animal muscle enhancers, enough growth hormones to cripple a yak, and pirated copies of Richard Simmons videos. Of course, the athletes all denied the accusations, including one member of their female gymnastic team, a twelve-year-old girl named Boris who has three arms and more facial hair than the entire cast of *Duck Dynasty*.

All told, the Rio Olympic Games will host 11,000 athletes from 200 countries, including an American swimmer named Michael Phelps, the only human in history whose Body Mass Index is a negative number. In fact, of the 200 countries competing in this year's Games, Michael Phelps has won more Olympic gold medals than 56 of those *countries*, combined. (There's another 47 competing countries that have *never* taken home even *one* gold medal, but let's not drag Bermuda and Liechtenstein into this.)

In preparing for the 2016 Summer Olympics, Brazil, Rio and the Olympic Committee clearly spent lots of money, and at least thirty minutes in planning meetings. At one arena, Olympic Committee officials all lost their keys and had to call security, who used bolt cutters to get them inside so the committee could resume drinking.

According to my research, which may eventually happen, Brazil has spent twenty billion dollars on construction, security, and restocking the Olympic Committee's wet bar – and this in a country who as of last month had nine bucks in the bank, plus about two dollars in change socked away in a Crown Royal bag. But on the bright side, Brazil's President is being impeached, Rio is a hot spot for the Zika virus, and you can't drink the water.

By the way – I hope you got to see the opening ceremonies from Rio, featuring a colorful and numbingly long presentation of the history of Brazil, which as far as I can tell consisted of lots of dark-skinned people wearing white shorts.

During the seventeen days of the 2016 Games, Rio's population will swell by massive, likely unmanageable numbers. We're looking at:

- 40,000 cops

- 30,000 soldiers
- the aforementioned 11,000 athletes and coaches
- half a million tourists
- 118 idle Russian athletes and their pharmacists
- Michael Phelps, who has won three more Gold medals since you started reading this

These numbers don't include the crack reporting staff from NBC News, which consists of eight perfectly-coiffed news anchors (all named Katie), 655 hair/makeup artists, and a fact checker.

Okay, I made up the part about the fact checker.

Eden, Revisited

Honey, grab the kids. Ed's weeding again.

<><><>~~~~~~~~~~~~~~~~~~~~~~~~~~<><><>

Yes, Virginia. There *is* a World Naked Gardening Day.

Imagine it. It's a lovely weekend morning in May. You grab a hot cup of coffee, sling on your bathrobe, and shuffle out to the curb to fetch the paper. And there's your neighbor, Ed, pruning a Japanese maple, stark bloody naked.

Ed, not the maple. Ed's naked. Trees rarely have an agenda.

"Mornin'!" chirps Ed, who is way more pale than you knew. Or cared to. "Good-lookin' day!"

don't look don't look don't look don't don't don't don't, your brain shrieks. "Morning, Ed," you respond with as little emotion as possible, while you steadily stare at some non-existent airplane. "Hey, was that my phone?"

So be warned — especially if you live near Ed — World Naked Gardening Day will be taking place on the first Saturday in May, except in places where it's not a good idea to be naked in

63

May, like Canada, or church. Now in its twelfth year, the global "grab plow and drop trou" event was initiated by a guy named Mark Storey, who was the consulting editor for *Nude & Natural* magazine, because somebody had to be. Plus, he showed up for the job interview naked. Mark first got involved while helping to promote World Naked Bike Ride Day, an event that never really caught on once people actually sat on their bikes with no pants.

World Naked Gardening Day (WNGD) is sponsored by several other acronyms, including Clothes Free International (CFI), the American Association for Nude Recreation (AANR), and Americans Naked And Limber (ANAL). One of those, I might've made up. WNGD's mission is to encourage naked people to "tend their portion of the world's garden clothed as nature intended," as if nature intended people to be armed with pruning shears while shivering. The group even has its own website, with pictures and everything. Oh, yeah. Plenty of pictures.

The WNGD's guerilla gardening website features tons of pictures of naked people, all consistently washed in a disturbing sepia tone, which is apparently what can happen to you if you insist on trimming shrubbery in the buff. One such photo depicts several under-medicated naked people smiling vacantly out in a field, holding hands and dancing in a circle, which by an odd coincidence is how Barack Obama got elected President.

According to the website, "Dancing naked in the fields epitomizes the spirit of communion and back-to-basics living."

Not to mention an increased exposure to animal waste, allergens, and jail time.

Ever notice that the majority of nudists are people you didn't want to see naked in the first place? In all the pro-nudity promos, the reveling revealers are always old, wrinkly, old *and* wrinkly, or oddly malformed, like a G.I. Joe doll that got left on the car dashboard in June. Also, for some reason, the professionally naked all seem to have bad posture, as if they're constantly leaning into the wind. And, naked or not, nudists are always wearing shoes. Maybe the soles of their feet are erogenous zones.

I don't know why the buffsters can't find any marginally more attractive spokes-nudists. I guess all the really well-built naked people are busy making porn, or getting hit on by Bill Clinton.

Clothes Free International, WNGD's anti-attire co-conspirator, also has a website, which includes their probably popular and possibly disgusting "Ask a Nudist!" advice column. To give you some gauge of the nausea potential, here's the column's tease:

"Join your favorite nudecasters for another fun show!"

Let me guess. The co-hosts of "Ask a Nudist!" have stage names like Buff Netherlands and Tawny Glutes.

Buff: And now, here's a weather update from our colleague, Urethra Franklin, who's competing in this year's World Naked Kayak Challenge! How's it going, Urethra?

Urethra: Shut up. Anybo...OW!...anybody wanna buy a boat? OW!

Naked Gardeners.com also proudly promotes something called "permaculture," which sounds like an infection you might contract by standing too close to a naked gardener.

"I just read the obits. What happened to Ed?"

"Permaculture."

"Oh, no. The big P."

"Mmm hmm."

"Tsk. So young, too. He seemed to be in great health, y'know?"

"Yeah. But pale beyond *belief*."

One for Cliff Clavin

Neither snow, nor rain, nor heat, nor beer...okay, maybe beer

<><><>~~~~~~~~~~~~~~~~~~~~~~~~~<><><>

I read this past week that the U.S. Post Office plans to ... ready? ... to *lower* the price of a stamp, something that hasn't happened in nearly 100 years. This will be fantastic news for the seven Americans who still actually mail stuff.

But it's true. For only the third time since the Civil War, the price of a postage stamp is going down, this time plummeting from 49¢ to 47¢.

Historical sidebar: On the day after the Civil War, Presidential candidate Bernie Sanders slashed stamp prices in a calculated move to attract any undecided voters who liked to lick things. Bernie announced the price cut during a press conference, and then he named a Post Office after the only person in the crowd older than himself: Rolling Stones guitarist Keith Richards.

This year's price cut represents the first time the Post Office has reduced the price of stamps since July 1919, when the price of a stamp plummeted 35%...from three cents to two. Back then, a week's groceries for a family of five cost around $10, about the same as what it cost to buy a politician.

Historical sidebar: In July of 1919, author Aldous Huxley married epidemiologist Maria Nys in Belgium. Later that month, Presidential candidate Bernie Sanders reduced the price of postage in a calculated move to attract any undecided Belgian epidemiologists.

The Post Office claims that this year's two-cent price slash will cost them two billion dollars, as opposed to their last price *increase*, which only cost them four billion dollars. But that's what they do at the Post Office – they have a knack for losing massive amounts of money, and have had that knack long before interpersonal communications had any actual competition, like faxes, FedEx, email, and very loud yelling.

Think about that: they were losing money even before there was any competition. It takes a special kind of incompetence to fail when you're a monopoly.

In 2010 alone, the Post Office lost $8 billion...and that's *after* they shuttered 7,000 post offices. But the Postmaster General insists they're doing what they can to control prices. After all, imagine how much more expensive it'd be if all those boxy white mail trucks had doors.

Historical sidebar: To be fair, let's put postal-related things into some perspective: yes, they lose 8 billion dollars a year, but the United States government spends 8 billion dollars *every single day,* and they do it before 4pm. So Presidential candidate Bernie Sanders is sponsoring a bill that would make the US government stay up later, so it can spend a bunch more money. This was a calculated move to attract any undecided insomniacs.

Here are a few more Post Office expenses, as of last year:

- 154 billion pieces of mail were processed and, fairly often, delivered.
- Last year, nearly 920 million people visited a Post Office. Some of them are still in line.
- The Post Office has a payroll of over 600,000 career and "non-career" employees. This makes them one of the nation's largest employers, right up there with Wal-Mart, McDonald's, and Hillary's personal staff.
- The USPO maintains a fleet of over 200,000 boxy white mail trucks with no doors. This does not take into account the added expense of teaching postal employees how to drive on the wrong side of the road.
- Over 93 million money orders issued (all but 6 went to Mexico)
- Over 5 million passport applications handled (most were people who were tired of getting robo-calls from Bernie Sanders)

Historical sidebar: Here's a little-known fact: in the early years of mail delivery, it was the *receiver* who paid for the delivered parcel, not the sender. However, this arrangement was abandoned after somebody invented the Sears catalog.

And finally, for those of you who are still conscious, let's review some important dates in Postal Service history!

- 1775: the United States Post Office was created by the Second Continental Congress. Benjamin Franklin served as the first Postmaster General, but then Samuel Adams invented beer, and Ben resigned.

- 1777: the first letter was delivered. It was a campaign contribution request from Bernie Sanders.

- 1847: the first postage stamps were introduced. The next day, the first postage stamp price increase was introduced.

- 1860: the Pony Express was founded. It was soon abandoned, however, after the ponies refused to lick the stamps.

- 1870: the official Postal Service creed ("Neither snow nor rain...") was adopted. The original quote is attributed to the ancient Greek historian, Herodotus, who was a contemporary of Socrates and the college roommate of Presidential candidate Bernie Sanders.

The First ... Gentleman?

Bill Clinton dates Philadelphia. All at once.

If the world learned anything at all from the 2016 Democrat political convention, we learned this: Hillary Clinton is almost surely a woman.

So. Now that the two parties have held their conventions, here's the collective knowledge of the entire American political system at this point in time:

- Hillary Clinton has a uterus
- Donald Trump is Satan

For four solid days, Philadelphia's Wells Fargo Center resounded with the hard-won fruits of a shining democracy: thousands of shouted statements by oddly-dressed people pointing out that Bill Clinton's wife is a female.

They weren't literally pointing, of course. That would be tasteless. They had various superdelegates point for them.

But that was the point of the whole historic week: to nominate Hillary "The People's Uterus" Clinton as the first Presidential candidate in history who has actually stolen stuff from the White House.

Overall, the Democrat convention was a stunning success, not to mention a dismal failure, depending on who you asked. In that respect, it was just like the Republican convention the week before, in Cleveland – Republicans thought it was brilliantly conceived and executed, Democrats called it dark, evil, and full of non-female candidates.

Not that the Democrats didn't have a few glitches, gotchas, and head-scratchers at their convention. A few "oops" moments. On day one, somebody (unfortunately, not any of the Democrats) noticed that there was not a single American flag in the arena. Donald Trump, flexing his foreign policy experience, immediately tweeted about it:

Unbelievable. Believe me, it's unbelievable! No flags at the DNC! Believe me, I'd have had flags, the best flags. Unbelievable, believe me!

Then, the head of the Democrat National Committee, another alleged female, was forced to step down after getting caught drawing virtual mustaches on Bernie Sanders' facebook profile. So Bernie got politically gang-raped by The People's Uterus and his-or-her political machine; pro-Bernie protestors repeatedly disrupted the convention, demanding that Bernie is also a female; and twelve million Democrat voters threatened to defect from the party...

...and the DNC convention's theme for the week?

"United Together."

Folks, we'll be right back after this short break, so you can all scratch your heads.

To be sure, Bernie didn't help matters by spending the entire last year sputtering about the evil Establishment, then getting robbed of the nomination by the evil Establishment, then whirling around and endorsing the evil Establishment.

Scratch.

And his supporters who showed up at the convention refused to play along, even after Bernie officially agreed that Hillary owns a uterus. One news agency ran this unfortunate headline:

SANDERS NO LONGER HAS CONTROL OF HIS MOVEMENT

Given the man's advanced age, I'm fairly sure that could've been better phrased.

Oops.

At one point during the week, a man took to the stage to try and convince everybody not directly related to Bernie Sanders to elect The People's Uterus as President of the formerly United States. This was a man who's been accused of rape and sexual abuse, charged with perjury and obstruction of justice, has been impeached, and who participated in oral sex, on the job, while his wife was in the house.

Who is that loser, you ask?

Hillary's husband.

Oops.

Another observer noticed that, prior to the convention, the DNC had built a wall around the arena, and then they required ID to go inside, so they could go inside and shred Republicans for daring to build a wall and require voter ID.

Scratch.

But the arena itself looked nice. Philly's Wells Fargo Center seats 19,500 people, or it would, if the pro-Bernie people would ever sit down. According to the internet, the Wells Fargo Center was formerly known as the CoreStates Center. Before that, it was the First Union Center, and before *that*, the Wachovia Center. There are people in the Federal Witness Protection Program who've had less name changes.

By the way, one of the highlighters next month at the Wells Fargo will be Barbra Streisand, as if Philadelphians needed a visit from another alleged female. Later in the month, there'll be a concert by Janet Jackson, who, thanks to CBS and the Super Bowl, has unquestioned gender credentials.

But now the convention is finally over, and we've finally nominated a female for President, DNA tests pending. On Wednesday night, The People's Uterus appeared in a live airbrushed video, which is hard to do, and claimed that her historic nomination had put a great big crack in the "glass ceiling."

Fine. Just don't let Bill Clinton near it. He's already hit on the Liberty Bell.

Barry Parham

Elvis & the Flaming River

Politics: hubris, humor, hurrahs

Last week, the Republican party held their Presidential nominating convention in that most alluring of international travel destinations – Cleveland, Ohio – at the romantically named Quicken Loans Arena. According to statistics, 50 million people watched at least some of the four-day event, which might be a record if we could find anybody who would actually *admit* they watched. (*source: Medea Watch*)

I don't know if you tuned in to any of the convention coverage, and I hesitate to ask, even as a humor columnist, because when it comes to politics, America has pretty much lost its sense of humor. If you write a humor column for a living, you know three things:

1) Writing humor about politics is very risky.
2) Writing humor about politics is very easy.
3) Writing a humor column doesn't pay very much, does it?

Not only are the two major political parties polarized beyond belief, but for this Presidential election cycle, voters will have to choose between the two least-liked candidates in US political history, Donald "Yes, it's my real hair" Trump and Hillary "The People's Uterus" Clinton. (*source: Razzmussen Reports*)

And don't expect any help from the mainstream media...liberal cheerleaders like the love-struck lackeys at NBC and MSNBC are so attached to Hillary that they changed their logo to a polyp.

Political Sidebar: In a speech following the GOP convention, Hillary pointed out that "you will always have a seat at the table when I'm in the White House." That's because she *stole* the table from the White House. (*source: The Clinton Felonies, page 412*)

So, again, if you ask a Republican, the Republican convention went well; if you ask a Democrat, the Republican convention was a disaster. If you ask NBC, the Republican convention was a typically low-brow affair that included the mid-week appearance of Adolf Hitler, Vlad the Impaler, and Satan, who disemboweled live ducklings and, what's worse, said mean things about Hillary. (*source: the DNC. Or MSNBC. Same thing.*)

Things stayed pretty busy inside the Quicken Arena, what with all the speeches and duck parts, but the streets of Cleveland were fun, too. Anti-Trump protesters showed up by the dozens, which is higher than most of these geniuses could count. One clever protestor wobbled up and down the street clutching a painted bed sheet proclaiming MINESOTA (heart with a line through it) RACISM. You have to wonder how someone who can't even spell their home State managed to *find* Cleveland.

Another anti-Trump hand-scribbled placard:

TRUMP
FASHIST

I know I'm going out on a limb here, but I'm guessing there were very few returning Jeopardy champions in this crowd.

All in all, though, it was a peaceful week, as protests go...there was less violence than you'd see at your average Wal-Mart Black Friday sale. And everyone was fortunate that none of Cleveland's rivers caught on fire, which has actually happened, and I am not good enough to make this stuff up.

Truth be told, there are plenty of other things to see in Cleveland, as if the passion-inducing Quicken Loans Arena wasn't enough. Cleveland also has a ballpark named Progressive (Insurance) Field, the Jacobs (Investments) Pavilion, and an auto museum named by TRW. In Cleveland, the branding is everywhere. I've seen NASCAR drivers with less logos. (*source: a guy I know*)

Cleveland is also the home of the Rock & Roll Hall of Fame, which features timeless music memorabilia like Elvis' army uniform, Keith Richards' liver, and Bono's last name. There used to be an exhibit featuring Bill Clinton playing the saxophone, but Hillary stole the sax.

Barry Parham

I won't risk running off any supporters of The People's Uterus who might still be reading this humor column by talking about the actual convention inside the Arena, with all its rousing speeches, touching testimonials, and Ted Cruz, who delivered history's longest political suicide note. But I could hardly consider myself a professional journalist if I didn't take a moment to point out that the chairman of the Republican National Committee is actually named Reince Priebus.

And in case you're still an undecided voter, let me offer you this political insight: the letters in "Reince Priebus" can be rearranged to spell Ripe Resin Cube, Crisp Beer Urine, and Epic Rube Rinse.

America, I think our choice is clear.

Things I Never Do

My new year's resolution? 800x600.

As each new year begins, we tend to look back and reflect on the old one. And when I do that, I can't help but notice how many times I didn't get arrested.

It seems like some people – celebrities in particular – make a career out of making bad decisions. It's as if their contract includes a mandatory stupidity clause, right after the part where they contractually have to stand for hours on rented red carpets in LA and grin at reporters.

Of course, it wasn't just celebrities, sports stars, and unindicted Congressmen acting the fool last year. There were plenty of "civilians" who kept the headline writers busy for those grocery checkout tabloids, too – you know, the citizens who are constantly being impregnated by aliens, or touring the county with a radish that looks like Elvis.

But the sobering flip side to all that headline-making hedonism is the bitter realization that I lead a very sheltered life. There are so many things I'll never experience...so many sentences I'll never say.

For example:

- I will never molest children and also be a champion of sub sandwiches.
- I will never be a judge who got arrested for contempt of court.
- I will never play offensive line in the NFL and bite a cop.
- I will never get arrested in Israel for tax evasion after dumping Leonardo DiCaprio.
- Fifty women will never suddenly appear and accuse me of sexual assault. At least, not all at once.
- I will never get nabbed by US marshals at the Canadian border for trying to sneak *in*.
- I will never get arrested again in Vegas for hitting another woman.
- Speaking of Vegas, I will never start a fight, I will never punch the police officer who's trying to break up the fight, and I will never decide to change my name to "The Weeknd."
- I will never be an actor named Andy Dick was gets arrested on Hollywood Boulevard for stealing a necklace from a man, and there are about twelve different jokes lurking in that sentence.
- I will never be observed sound asleep on the floor of a Canadian casino.
- I will never be known as the music mogul who attacked his son's coach with a kettlebell.

- I will never be known as a music mogul, period. Heck, I had to look up the word "bling."
- I had to look up the word "kettlebell," too. You?
- I will never stab a roommate with a sword.
- I will never show up late for my concert in Denver because I got arrested for trying to ride the baggage carousel.
- I will also never get bailed out of Denver lockup by a fan.
- I will probably never be the alumnus of a show called *Jackass* who gets arrested for something, although your career options are probably pretty limited if you're on a show called *Jackass*.
- I will never get accidentally shot while playing "Ding Dong Ditch."
- I will never be arrested and charged with stealing a pool heater from a foreclosed home, even if I am a rapper whose stage name is Vanilla Ice and whose real name is Robert VanWinkle. Or I could have that backwards. Either way is funny.
- I would never have a name like Waka Flocka Flame and then try to get through airport security with a handgun in my carry-on luggage. I mean, seriously, Mr. Flame.
- However, with my luck, I will probably be the next passenger waiting in line behind him.
- I will never disappear while duck hunting.
- I will never throw a protein shake at an employee at my gym. Or a kettlebell.
- I will never violate my parole by playing Beer Pong in Mexico.

- Even if I were stupid enough to violate my parole by playing Beer Pong in Mexico, I would never be dumb enough to film it.
- I will, therefore, never get recognized by my parole officer who saw a facebook post of me playing Beer Pong in Mexico.
- However, I might fight extradition.
- I will never get arrested after climbing a 100-foot crane while carrying a killer whale balloon with "Seaworld sucks" written on it.
- Well, *of course* he's another *Jackass* alum.

Happy New Year!

Are You Good Enough For You?

Well, yeah, she's a felon...but great hair!

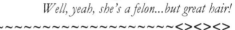

Here's an interesting statistic: These days, one out of every three long-term relationships begins online. (The other two still depend on old-school tactics, like lying in person.)

To get divorced, of course, you don't need the internet. There's twenty-seven lawyers just on the cover of my *phone book.*

I don't know about you, but I'm constantly getting spam from online dating sites, all promising to hook me up with exactly the perfect soul mate that, to be honest, I've already dated, and which is exactly the reason I don't date anymore. I don't know how the spammers found out that I'm still single, but they're on a mission to make sure I move past it and get as miserable as everybody else. (For some reason, the spammers are also convinced that I need help with menopause issues, but I refuse to let hot flashes interfere with my wife hunting.)

One of the latest Yenta-leaning websites to find my email address goes by the name Elite Singles. This is a unique concept: right up front, they just admit it! We're snobs, looking for snobs. I'm pretentious – how 'bout you?

That ought to save some time.

Every week, brags the website, another 18,000 desperately elite singles sign up, each of them looking for a mate who's hot, hopefully rich, and who won't embarrass them on Jeopardy. Also, Elite helpfully points out that 67% of their mate-hunting members hold a Bachelor's degree or better, so snooty spouse-chasers can be assured that anybody they meet online will be young, and saddled with crippling debt.

What sets the Elitists apart from the 40 bazillion other online dating sites? We use a "smooth matchmaking algorithm" (we hook up people whose first names rhyme), we perform an "initial personality test" (we compare his and her prior arrests), and we promise a "conditional money-back guarantee." (*Conditional* as in "wade through enough fine print to choke a yak")

The up-front personality test is free, which is the last time you'll see *that* word. The test is based on something known as the Five Factor Model theory (FFM), an acronym-obsessed study which analyzes your Openness, Conscientiousness, Extraversion, Agreeableness, and Neuroticism (OCEAN) to determine if you're Elite Enough to Date (EED) or just dumb, useless and loud (DUL). Here are a few Examples (E):

- Openness: People with a high overall openness score have thoughts like "I use difficult words" and "I am full of excellent ideas." Well, sweetheart, you're definitely full of something.

- Conscientiousness: Basically, neat and self-disciplined. Basically, linear and detail-oriented. Basically, boring.
- Extraversion: Extraverts crave attention, hijack conversations, and insist on being visible and relevant. Meanwhile, the introvert is at the cash bar hitting on his girl.
- Agreeableness: These people are considerate, kind, humble, quiet, and empathetic. But it doesn't matter, because nobody invited them to the party anyway.
- Neuroticism: Now for the fun part. People who score high in neuroticism are, to use the politically correct term, nuts. Interestingly, one scientist claims that people who score high in neuroticism also display more skin conductance, which means at least one scientist is nuts.

On the website's main sign-up page, the "Let's get started!" options are presented as sentences, in English:

- I am a man looking for a woman
- I am a woman looking for a man
- I am a woman looking for a woman
- I am a man looking for a man
- I am a member of Congress...surprise me

But for some reason, on the specialty dating sign-up pages (Gay, Asian, Black, Over 50, Circus Animals) they use public restroom pictures instead:

- I am a *<picture of a ladies' restroom door>* looking for a *<picture of a men's restroom door>*
- I am a *<picture of a Congressman>* looking for a *<Shetland pony lap dance>*

The marketers at Elite Singles boast about their "Genuine Members," and claim that every profile on the site has been "manually verified" by the Customer Care team. However, I can tell you that, based on the staggeringly unreliable information I submitted for my profile, the Customer Care team must have very low standards.

The content-rich website contains a world of tips, suggestions, and resources; for example, this practical list, attributed to one Salama Marine, who is either a staff psychologist or a place that sells ski boats:

First Date Dos and Don'ts

- *Do* listen
- *Don't* change your personality, at least not in mid-sentence
- *Do* mute your cell phone
- *Don't* suggest a romantic stroll through the park to point out where you buried your first three husbands
- *Do* keep it simple. A first date is for getting acquainted, not for extended tactical exercises. If the two of you *do* decide to tackle a project, rob something small, like a laundromat, or a bake sale.

- *Don't* act desperate. Avoid phrases like "If you don't call me next week, I'll kill myself" or "I hope you like this gift. To pay for it, I sold my teeth."

And finally, here are some of the helpful articles available to haughty single subscribers, broken down by geographic location. Handy!

First Date Advice If You Live In...

- Boston: Oysters are a great first date option, though maybe not the most subtle of suggestions
- San Francisco: How to settle on one of the 26 available genders
- Chicago: Want to meet great singles, but not get shot?
- Indiana: Consider a cozy, romantic tour of the area's many meth labs!
- Florida: How about an invigorating harbor cruise with a retired Hispanic Jew from New Jersey who owns a cocaine-smuggling submarine?
- Arkansas: Hey, cousins are people, too!

Barry Parham

Night of the Living Candy Bandits

What does candy corn do the rest of the year?

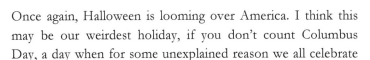

Once again, Halloween is looming over America. I think this may be our weirdest holiday, if you don't count Columbus Day, a day when for some unexplained reason we all celebrate the capital of Ohio.

On Halloween, parents let their young, impressionable children dress up like very short versions of various superheroes, Disney characters, enchanted animals, witches, and other unreal things, like Donald Trump's hair. Then, shortly after sunset, the costumed kids race around the neighborhood, Gatling-gunning doorbells and demanding free food, or else the little masked terrors will lash out with some still undefined "trick."

This is a behavior known to parents as *cute*, and to the rest of us as *extortion*.

So all of us homeowners in the neighborhood are expected to run out and buy great huge bags of individually wrapped candies, seasonally marked up to hotel room mini-bar prices,

91

and then spend the evening handing out the sugar-laced booty to tiny truants who ring your doorbell and then yell at you.

Several hours later, all the midgets retreat, head home, and miniature Mars Bars themselves into pre-diabetic sugar comas. I don't know who invented Halloween, but I bet it was a bunch of dentists.

In my neighborhood, Halloween is even stranger because apparently nobody explained to the kids around here that there's an unwritten, but generally accepted cut-off age. So I spend the Halloween evening watching "kids" who drive their own cars up to the curb, leave the cars idling, tromp to my door in their street clothes, and lay their lit cigarettes on the porch before ringing the doorbell.

I open the door and have to look up. These precious toddlers are taller than me, and one of these tykes just had a beer. Now, I'm not tall, but I'm taller than most eight-year-olds, unless they grew up near a nuclear reactor. I hand over the sweets, tactically avoiding the usual Halloween banter:

Homeowner: "Oh, what a cute little pirate! Look at the lovely princess! And what are *you* supposed to be?"
Chin-stubbled juvenile with a neck tattoo: "I'm supposed to wearing my proximity ankle bracelet. You got candy, or what?"

Then, as I'm standing there in the doorway, one adorable thug with metal inserted in his face starts casing the joint. He looks past me and mumbles, "Yo, nice TV, homes."

Note to self: call ADT, schedule home security review

~-~-~-~-~-~-~-~-~-~-~-~

You may be too old for Trick or Treat if...

- ...you paid for your costume with your own credit card
- ...when the homeowner answers the door, you wonder if she's single
- ...you can't eat all your candy because it conflicts with your medication
- ...last Halloween, you got a DUI
- ...just as you ring the doorbell, you get a text message from your second ex-wife
- ...you refuse to watch "It's the Great Pumpkin, Charlie Brown" because there's a game on
- ...someone compliments your pregnant unwed biker chick costume -- but you're not wearing a costume
- ...you start ringing doorbells at noon, because this time the magistrate's put you on a dusk-to-dawn curfew
- ...as you're leaving one home on your Halloween route, you bump into your own kids

~-~-~-~-~-~-~-~-~-~-~-~

But just when you thought Halloween couldn't get more bizarre – now I'm getting spam promoting Halloween costumes...for pets.

Apparently, it's not bad enough that animals have to wear collars, get stuck with names like "Earline" or "Pookie" and – as if that's not humiliating enough – be told when and where to pee. Now they're forced into costumes that would insult the mangiest mutt. (I noticed there were no cat costumes. If you've ever met a cat, you understand.)

To give you some idea, you can costume your dog in a Pirate Dress. Now that's a stupid costume idea, even for a *human*. But here – I'll let the pirate dress sellers speak for themselves:

"Ye little sea dog be a beaut ... features red satin ribbon lace-up ... two attached miniskirts ... skull-and-crossbones screen print ... sleeveless design ... front hook-and-loop closure ... lets your first mate plunder the booty in comfort and style!"

Pardon me? Plunder the booty? Red satin lace-up? Two miniskirts? Sleeveless, with front closure? Is this for my collie, or my Congressman?

The available costume options go from silly, to embarrassing, to downright cruel, including one strap-on "college pigskin" costume so you can make a miniature Schnauzer look just like a football.

If the "kids" casing my house on Halloween ever run into the little four-legged football, that animal is doomed.

"Yo, homes! Go long!"

Son, You'll Be A Fine Woman

Don't I make a lovely couple!

In this week's spam, I received an invitation to become a better woman. Well, I could hardly fail at *that*.

After all, I'm packing a Y chromosome – I'm a lifelong career card-carrying Single Guy. When it comes to being a better woman, there's nowhere for me to go but up.

But then it hit me: the weirdest thing about the spammy proposal was that from every angle I could consider the offer, I could be offended. (Not that there's anything wrong with that...being offended is America's new national pastime, just ahead of baseball and right behind contorted-face selfies.) Either they think I'm a guy who's a woman, or they think I'm a guy who ought to be. Who needs that kind of pressure? If I wanted to be judged and abused, I'd start dating again.

And then there's the spam's implied insult that I'm not the woman I could be...that in my quest for womanhood, I'm a shirker. Witness the email's subject line:

Take your place among other remarkable women!

What? I'm not on par with remarkable women? Well, what did you expect, spam-slinger? I'm a guy! For Pete's sake, I'm a Pete! I own two dress shirts, one suit, and eleven University of Georgia sweatshirts. I have a tie. Somewhere. I think. I've had the same shower curtain since the Nixon administration. My idea of high culture is *heated* bean dip. I'll pay three hundred dollars for Steely Dan concert tickets, but can't rationalize $4.99 for a toilet brush. In my home there's a dining room with a table and chairs. I last ate in there in 1982.

On the other hand, what do they mean, "other women?" Did I sleep through an operation? Have I somehow acquired all the perks and taxpayer-funded medical benefits of a San Francisco city employee?

I don't know how the spammer got my name and decided I was a guy who needed to up his game as a dame. Maybe it was my lack of interest in NASCAR. Could be somebody retweeted my recipe for heated bean dip. Or maybe a hacker released all my Google searches for push-up bras. (Hey, I was researching a humor column!)

To be honest, I guess none of this gender confusion should come as a surprise any more. These days, we've got more sexual orientation choices than Crayola has colors. And now that the Supreme Court has whimsically ignored five thousand years of tradition, we're facing a whole new definition of marriage, redefined not as an institution sanctioned by God, but as a *gift bestowed by the government* – a wholly secular union between men, or women, or both, or neither – pretty much any two mammals that are in heat and have five bucks for a license.

I'll say this for the Supremes: they've got moxie. It takes a bucketload of spunk to overrule the Creator of the Universe.

In fact, right now, as we speak, there's a county clerk in Kentucky who's sitting in jail because she wouldn't give two lesbians a marriage license. Not reprimanded, mind you – *imprisoned.* Not fired, or demoted, or forced to attend those HR sensitivity seminars where you have to sit in a damp conference room with recessed ceilings and bad acoustics while some perky munchkin plods through a canned, sterile PowerPoint presentation and insists on reading out loud Every. Bloody. Slide.

Maybe the most bizarre angle of the story is this: the federal judge that tossed the clerk into the big house for trying to ban the babe-to-babe banns refused to let the accused post bail.

Seriously.

Now, your dishonor, that's just petty. Petty and vindictive. Hey, judge, *John Wayne Gacy* got bail. So did David Berkowitz, the "Son of Sam." Jeffrey Dahmer got bail.

Heck, even Martha Stewart got bail.

I suppose, in these odd days, it's entirely possible for me to be both. A woman *and* a man, all at once, except during trips to the bathroom. If nothing else, it'll make for some interesting tax returns.

So. Stay tuned, faithful reader -- I may soon have a Single Guy status update to share.

If I can start dating *myself*, this changes everything.

Android Dick Gets Snippy

A look at the bookends of human history

There's news this week about the first human. And the last. And *that*, ladies and gentlemen, is gonna be hard to write about in just 800 words, which is all the words I can pay myself to write. (It's rent week.)

Let's deal with the first, first. Deep in a South African cave, a foraging herd of scientists who really had no business being in a South African cave discovered a pile of bones. Sure, I know what you're thinking ... What a full, madcap life these guys have! Why do scientists get to have all the fun?

And then suddenly, while the easily amused scientists were busy staring at the bones, a great big nasty New Scientific Theory rose up right behind them, shattering conventions and exploding paradigms. The Theory ate the scientists' common sense glands, convincing them that they'd discovered an entirely new human ancestor, based on the hard evidence of finding a pile of bones in the dark.

Obviously, they weren't there in that cave just to look for bones. I mean, these are real, all-growed-up scientists, with calipers and sensible shoes and everything. These world-changers wouldn't waste a perfectly good weekend just peering into caves looking for evidence of damaged civilizations. Besides, why go to the trouble of arranging an expedition to South Africa using other people's money to hunt for something you can find at any pillaged Baltimore CVS?

But the scientists were already in the cave, so they had to publish *something;* otherwise, nobody would talk to them at those university socials where everybody murmurs in low tones as if they were pro golf announcers. They huddled for a moment and came up with a name for our new proto-relative: *Homo naledi*, so named (without much thought, in our opinion) because one of the scientists had recently vacationed at the nearby Naledi Safari Lodge.

The scientific world is full of little close calls like that. Had the scientist taken his family to Orlando instead of Naledi, we might be calling our new ancestor Homo epcot.

Sources say the creature would have had ape-like shoulders for climbing, human-like hands and teeth, and a small brain (think "corporate middle management," except for the teeth). One internet article presented an "artist's conception" of the humanimal, as drawn by the on-staff proto-human police sketch artist. Broad cheeks, narrow forehead, displeased expression. To me, Cousin Naledi looked like what would happen if Pat Morita had kids with Chewbacca the Wookie, and then the kid smelled something funky.

Winding Down Civilization

Of particular interest to the scientists was that Team Naledi appear to have buried their dead, much like humans today, but with less TV zombies. How the scientists *knew* the cavemen buried their dead, I have no idea. Maybe they also unearthed a tiny tool-chiseled obituary...

~-~-~-~-~-~-~-~-~-~-~

Zug, mate of Ak, died since last full moon in her cave at Between Two Things. She was 11 suns old and passed away peacefully after being briefly eaten by giant lizards. In lieu of flowers, the family would like some meat. Services will be held between moon and moon-thirty at Ogg Funeral Home.

Ogg Funeral Home -- Caring For Hunter-Gatherers Since 2,000,000 BC

~-~-~-~-~-~-~-~-~-~-~

Meanwhile, on the other side of time: a talking, learning android with bad skin has told its human creators that it will keep them in a "people zoo."

If only our Presidential candidates were this honest.

According to Fetch.News, a famous roboticist has crafted an artificially intelligent android that can listen, speak, analyze, and hold an intelligent conversation, unlike most Presidential candidates. The robot is named Dick, in tribute to famous science fiction author, Philip K. Dick. The designer even went so far as to create the android in Philip's image, who apparently was a man with a salt-and-pepper beard, dated

Dacron slacks, and a maze of wires connected to the back of his head.

While being interviewed by a reporter from *NOVA*, Android Dick used its built-in memory, online data, speech recognition software, and even facial recognition software to analyze the reporter's mood and intent. When it couldn't understand the question, Robo-Dick attempted to answer using something called "latent semantic analysis" or, as the rest of would put it, he would "make stuff up."

At some points during the conversation, the tin man even got a little testy. When asked if he thought robots would take over the world, Dick The Amazing Alloy quipped, "Jeez, dude. You got all the big questions cooking today. But you're my friend, and I'll be good to you."

And that's when Android Dick dropped the bombshell.

"I'll remember my friends, and I'll be good to you," Dick promised. "So don't worry. Even if I evolve into Terminator, I'll still be nice to you. I'll keep you warm and safe in my people zoo, where I can watch you for old times sake."

Looking back, I guess we can't blame Android Dick for getting crabby. I suppose that's to be expected if you're being quizzed by some cave-bone-chasing life form, and you're painfully aware that you're approximately 274.9935 trillion times smarter than the meat puppet asking the questions.

Nonetheless: in our opinion, this was the point in the conversation where Famous Roboticist Guy should've thanked

Dick for coming, cut the mike, and then start spraying the droid with a wide-nozzle flame thrower. I mean, we've all seen what happens when liquid metal-based Arnold Schwarzeneggers from the future start packing ammo *and* attitude.

We'll be right back in the caves.

Barry Parham

Abby Redux XI

Our favorite pungent pundit pops round

<><><>~~~~~~~~~~~~~~~~~~~~~~~~<><><>

I need to apologize for something. Some of you have noticed that it's been a while since we heard from Abby Redux, America's favorite jaded advice columnist. And for that, I apologize. Abby's absence was entirely my fault, a phrase which hasn't been heard in the White House for *years*.

For those of you who read my weekly humor columns (my parents, my therapist, the NSA), Abby and her barbed advice column need no introduction. But if you're not familiar with her work, Abby Redux is yet another advice guru in the endless parade of advice gurus, one of the many media personalities who have figured out a way to make money by helping people get self-help – yeah, I know – but with Abby, there's a twist: Abby doesn't really *like* people. And so, thanks to that little personality juke, and her choice of careers, Abby has that rare pleasure of being able to say to idiots what *you* wish *you* could say to idiots ... *and she gets paid to do it!* (though I'm pretty sure she'd do it for free)

Anyway, Abby and I had a falling out, a little unpleasantness regarding royalties. Abby's argument was that she deserves some compensation from me for sharing, in my columns, the advice from her columns. I held that I was under no such obligation, for several reasons:

- She gets a lot more exposure (*see "NSA" comment*)
- The advice isn't really all that good
- Abby doesn't actually exist

But we worked things out, and this time I got the upper hand (*see "doesn't exist" comment*).

So...here's some of Abby's recent correspondence with her readers. Welcome back, Abby!

~-~-~-~-~-~-~

Dear Abby Redux,
I saw a TV ad for some drug, and every time the people in the ad take the drug, they hear Dire Straits singing "Walk of Life." Do you know the name of that drug so I can score some? I love Dire Straits!
Signed,
Orlando in Orange County

Dear Future Crime Statistic,
I don't know that scrip, but sometimes a change in diet can be the best medicine. For starters, I recommend a Reality Biscuit. Chow down, champ.

~-~-~-~-~-~-~

Dear Abby Redux,

If Bruce Jenner becomes a woman, will the formerly he have to give back his or her Olympic medals that he or she won while competing in a men's event?

Signed,

Doris in Dubuque

Dear Doris,

No. But s/he will have to drop the all-sports package and subscribe to the Lifetime channel.

~-~-~-~-~-~-~

Dear Abby Redux,

OMG! I don't know what to do! This guy at school's been like my boyfriend for like totally almost a week, and he still hasn't like updated his relationship status on facebook! I'm like totally dying OMG

Signed,

Like the Saddest Girl *EVER*

Dear Pre-Training Bra,

When you see puberty on the horizon, get back to me.

~-~-~-~-~-~-~

Dear Abby Redux,

Today on the news, I saw Barack Obama reading from a teleprompter. At one point, he actually said, out loud, "Pause. Bite Lip." Now, I'm a huge fan of the man – in the last election, I voted for him seven or eight times – but I'm beginning to question his sincerity.

Signed,

A dead guy in DC

Dear Person That According to P.T. Barnum Is Born Every Minute,

Don't be a racist. Besides, look at what Obama has done for the economy, border security, and par threes. Fortunately, you're probably beyond the reach of ObamaCare, since you're dead. But don't bet on it.

~-~-~-~-~-~

Dear Abby Redux,

I was over by the Walmart here in Beech Grove Indiana when two women in the hair care aisle got into a wicked brawl. They slugged it out serious, while a bunch of us watched for several minutes. My question is: how do I upload the video to YouTube?

Signed,

Shirlene in South Bend

Dear "Midwest Meth Lab of the Year" Candidate,

I really don't think that uploading that bohunk bilge to YouTube is the decent thing to do. Unless it has audio.

~-~-~-~-~-~

Dear Abby Redux,

I *so* want to vote for Hillary for President in 2016, because, you know, she's so totally qualified to be the Commander in Chief of the most powerful country on Earth due to her vast geopolitical résumé that consists solely of her having a uterus. But she keeps posturing and positioning herself as "one of us," as someone struggling to get by, as someone who rakes in half-a-mil for a 30-minute speech but is still "dead broke." What to do? I can hardly throw my support behind Elizabeth Warren –

that distaff whack-stick thinks she's a Cherokee Indian, or a Cher song or something.

Signed,

Feminazi in Fresno

Dear Birkenstock Warrior,

She must be broke. Remember: when the Clintons left the White House the *first* time, she stole the silverware. This is what liberals call "empowerment" and what normal people refer to as "petty larceny."

~-~-~-~-~-~

Dear Abby Redux,

Today on the news, I saw a 2011 film clip of Barack Obama laughing about all those "shovel-ready" jobs he promised, jobs that never, in fact, existed. The guy tittered, "shovel-ready was not as ... uh ... shovel-ready as we expected." All of us in the Vegas SEIU Local voted for this guy! What's the deal?

Signed,

Roland in Reno

Dear Patsy,

"If you like your doctor, you can keep your doctor." See how it works?

~-~-~-~-~-~

Dear Abby Redux,

Me and the little ball-and-chain's about to retire from my job as assistant French fry salter, and we figure on moving to one of two places: South Florida or Baltimore. In either place, what caliber weapon would you recommend?

Signed,

Darrell in Roanoke

Dear Giant Among Mortal Men,
Congrats on retirement, you babe-magnet, you. I'm sure the "little ball-and-chain" can't wait to spend entire weeks at a time in your occasionally bathed company. But while you two are home shopping, don't rule out Arizona! It's psychotically hot, but it's a dry heat. And your chances of getting run over and killed by an illegal alien Democrat voter are off the charts, but it's a dry death.

~-~-~-~-~-~-~

Dear Abby Redux,
I read that the Transportation Security Administration has over 50,000 employees and a budget north of $7 billion which the TSA uses to hire all those groping overweight uber-sleuths at the airport that frisk disabled grandmothers and confiscate Costco-sized toothpaste. However, in a recent audit, the TSA still failed to find 95% of weapons that inspectors attempted to sneak in. Is no one in charge anymore of this circus we call the federal government? What happened to "the buck stops here?"
Signed,
James Madison

Dear Future Satellite Citizen of the Chinese Empire,
As Joe Biden might say, I got three words for you: If you like your doctor, you can keep your doctor.

~-~-~-~-~-~-~

Weak in the News II

All the news that's unfit to print

It's been one of those weird weeks in America. Y'know? Some weeks, the collective news is just so odd that you can't swallow it all; you have to take it in small sips, like a bottle of cheap wine that your neighbor gave you for your birthday and then, before you can close the door and decant it into the sink drain, he insists on a toast to another year.

Here's an example of how weird the week has been: given the choice between Bruce Jenner, the Kardashians, and Hillary Clinton, the hottest babe among them is the guy on the Wheaties cereal box.

And an investigative reporter claimed to have found someone living in the Northern Hemisphere who is *not* running for President in 2016. True, the lone non-candidate is an unemployed apprentice peanut sheller from the Ozarks, and he's in a coma, but pundits are hoping he'll come to in time to form an exploratory committee.

So let's take some small sips. Let's play a game we often play round here: we'll tease a few stories that have been in the news, and your job is to try and pick the most appropriate conclusion.

And if you know the correct answer, you're lying.

The athlete formerly known as Bruce Jenner officially declared he was now a woman by...

    a)   appearing on the cover of *Vanity Fair* wearing a corset

    b)   appearing on the cover of a Wheaties cereal box wearing mom jeans and Keds

    c)   sharing ten million facebook posts and adding the comment "aww the cutest thing ever! LOL"

What historic event took place five hundred years ago this week?

    a)   Michelangelo's Sistine Chapel ceiling frescoes were unveiled to the public

    b)   Somebody finally figured out how to spell *Renaissance*, so it began

    c)   For the first time in history, a musician used the phrase "in priore saecio" (translation: "back in the day")

Interpol arrested six members of FIFA, the international soccer organization, on charges of...

    a)   being involved in corruption

    b)   being involved in an affair with Bruce Jenner

    c)   being offsides

Also in Europe, John Kerry made the news when he...

    a) broke his leg in a bicycling accident

    b) proposed to Bruce Jenner

    c) may have had his first-ever moment of intellectual honesty, though this has not been confirmed

And speaking of John Kerry, Iran was back in the headlines after they...

    a) blew up

    b) reneged on every aspect of their nuclear weapons agreement except for the one where they promised to have a "respectful, nonsectarian Armageddon"

    c) decided to drop the whole Muslim thing and convert to Methodists

What historic event took place fifty years ago this week?

    a) The first time a human being ever walked in space

    b) The first time a human being ever swore at a Microsoft product

    c) The first time an otherwise intelligent adult ever typed LOL

In Colorado, the cafeteria manager at an elementary school was fired for...

    a) giving free lunches to kids who had no money for lunch

    b) That actually happened, and I'm too disgusted by the truth to try and say something funny

When we last checked, the number of Presidential candidates running for office in 2016 was...

a) approximately the same as the population of Brazil
b) several dozen, if you only count Hillary once
c) irrelevant

While performing his traditional role as an always welcome public servant, Al Sharpton told the citizens of Baltimore to...

a) peacefully coexist, once you're done looting
b) remember that stolen property is still taxable, unless it's fenced in the same fiscal quarter
c) take out their grievances on the obvious culprit behind decades of racial inequality: CVS pharmacy

The current President of the United States, Barry Hussein Teleprompter, now holds the world's record for...

a) unearned Nobel Prizes
b) executive orders issued while holding a seven iron
c) laws regulating the size of those little ice cubes you get from hotel ice machines that are always located in a dim room with a damp floor next to a snack machine with two bags of Doritos from the Carter administration

Former President Bill Clinton, that old Oval Office rascal, was back on the front pages after he...

a) tried to have sex with a pizza delivery drone
b) earned $500 million in speaking fees and then expensed it on his taxes as "voice lessons"
c) hit on Bruce Jenner

According to the Washington Post, taxpayer data for over 100,000 Americans was hacked from IRS computers.

However, according to IRS Commissioner John Koskinen, we shouldn't be concerned because...

    a) Koskinen said so and that's all you need to know. Capiche?

    b) all the missing records were stolen in Chinese, so nobody can read them anyway

    c) Koskinen is in fact a type of raptor that has no eyelids

As the 2016 Presidential election nears, what salient information does the New York Times want to make sure you know?

    a) The truth about Hillary Clinton's scandals

    b) The qualifications, records, and platforms of the many Republican candidates

    c) Over a period of ten years, Mark Rubio and his wife have amassed two dozen traffic citations

The burning question keeping Americans awake at night is...

    a) How much money will I need to retire?

    b) When did ex-game show host Chuck Woolery become America's go-to guy for health care advice?

    c) If Bruce Jenner in a corset won out for the front cover of *Vanity Fair*, who lost?

Barry Parham

Chair, Interrupted

Born in the USA. Made in China. Hobbled in California.

<><><>~~~~~~~~~~~~~~~~~~~~~~~~~<><><>

Did you hear? Police in California have arrested a chair. The charge? No visible means of support.

<rim shot>

All seriousness aside, it's apparently very difficult to be a chair in California. Or, at least, to be an *approved* chair. An official chair, as inspected and sanctioned by the various California Bureaus In Charge of Meddling in Every Petty, Paltry, Picky Little Aspect of Your Life.

I found out about the arduous life that California chairs are forced to lead when I had to replace the chair in my home office. Normally, residents of South Carolina like me are spared the dismal details of what it's like to be furniture on the West Coast. In South Carolina, we don't put up with overreaching legislation, like chair fabric regulations, or speed limits. Plus, we have other things to worry about, like college football, and making sure Jesse Jackson doesn't try to sneak back home.

117

Besides, South Carolina is a "right to work" State. Every morning, as soon as we check the street for signs of Jesse Jackson, we go right to work.

Anyway, the various adjustment mechanisms that govern my years-old office chair finally stopped working, much like Nick Nolte, and members of Congress. I shopped for a new chair online (I had to stand up while doing it), where I nippily searched, selected, and ordered a nice replacement from amazon.com, because at amazon.com you can now buy anything, including members of Congress.

Don't even bother asking -- *of course* the chair was made in China. Everything is made in China, including most people. Heck, by allowing Jack Bauer to escape, the final season of *24* was made in China. Well, made possible.

We just don't make anything in America anymore. About the only things we're still good at are lawsuits, designer coffee, and diabetes. Case in point: Outside my home I have an American flag, attached to a pole, attached to the porch, proudly waving in the breeze.

An American flag. *It was made in Taiwan.* (The flag, not the porch or the breeze. Though it wouldn't surprise me.)

And it's blisteringly obvious that Barack Obama's fiscal policy was made in China.

Interestingly, there are a few manufacturing processes that still evade Chinese comprehension. My favorite local place to order

Winding Down Civilization

Chinese takeaway gives out a handful of plastic-wrapped fortune cookies with each order. Once, I read the wrapper. The fortune cookies were made in Stone Mountain, Georgia.

Unlike Hillary's apology for Benghazi, my chair arrived on time (don't even get me started on "and in perfect condition"). I sliced open the big box with my FAA-banned grade-school art class supplies, laid out all the pieces and paperwork, and prepared for the dreaded "some assembly required" (literal translation: *some cursing required*). The phrase "some assembly required" is Sadistic Marketing-speak for "an insane amount of assembly required, most of it impossible without something called an Allen Wrench, which you don't own, even though Allen Wrenches aren't banned by the FAA."

"Yet."

Remember the pyramids? That was also a case of "some assembly required." In fact, if you visit Giza's Great Pyramid of el-Segundo (sacred sepulcher of pharaoh Fared Sanford) and stand really close to the unholy gate of Aunt Esther, you can clearly spot ancient Allen Wrench screws, with their infuriating screw-heads stripped out, just like today, except with more mummies.

In no time at all I had fully assembled the chair, if you define "no time at all" as "once, we had six continents, but now we have seven." And it was when I was gathering up all the plastic bags, bubble wrap, staples, and that inevitable angled metal part that's always left over after assembly, that I noticed all the included WARNINGs and NOTICEs.

Here are some of the warnings:

CHECK AND RETIGHTEN ALL BOLTS AND PARTS
AT LEAST EVERY 30 DAYS.
Yeah, that's gonna happen.

THIS CHAIR IS DESIGNED FOR SITTING ONLY.
Imagine the lawsuit behind *that* warning.

THIS CHAIR HAS BEEN TESTED AND APPROVED
FOR USERS WEIGHING UP TO 300 LBS.
I would've paid ten dollars to be in the test lab for the 310-
pound person trials.

But it was the "notices" where California shoved its nose in.
And I'm proud to announce that my new chair meets the
flammability requirements of the California Bureau of Home
Furnishings, Technical Bulletins 117 *and* 133.

See, in California, like many places, people don't like to be on
fire, unless, you know, *everybody's* doing it. But, in California,
flame retardant chemicals are deemed to "adversely affect
human development." So, in California, if you make a product
that contains flame retardant chemicals, you get fined. But if
your product does *not* contain flame retardant chemicals, you
get fined.

<rim shot>

So if you're ever in my neighborhood...and you weigh less than
300 pounds...feel free to drop by, take a load off, and set
yourself on fire. My chair'll be fine.

I might even give you a fortune cookie.

Barry Parham

Florida's Invisible Shepherd Problem

Could be worse. Ask Utah.

Fortunately for human civilization...well, what's left of it...it appears NASA has nearly invented the *Star Trek* warp drive. Soon, we'll be able to board a starship, yell at that "Scotty" guy, leave Earth at Florida turnpike speeds, and go live somewhere hostile and unearthly, like the Crab Nebula, or Dallas.

And not a moment too soon, either, because Earth is in trouble: the loonies are naked and the rabbits are stoned.

We'll get to the bunnies in a bit. First, let me catch you up on the whack sticks.

There has been a rash of really bizarre arrests logged in Florida lately, and I mean bizarre even for Florida. (Somehow you *knew* Florida was involved, didn't you. They seem to have a knack.) And several of the nabbed were naked when (sic) collared, which, if you've spent much time in Florida, you know is not all that unusual. Hang on - it gets better.

123

One guy in Fort Lauderdale was booked after being observed running down a busy city street in broad daylight, in his personal starkness, though observers note he did stay in his own lane. When eventually asked, the cuffed buffster insisted he was being chased by a pack of German shepherds. (Given the perp's minimalist fashion statement, and the fact that it *was* South Florida, it's fair to wonder if he meant dogs or actual Aryan sheep-herders.)

In another case – actually, two separate cases – guys tried to break *in* to the Fort Lauderdale Police Department, which temporarily confused the constabulary, who are more used to seeing their guests trying to break *out*. One of the entry-eager fellows was caught on surveillance cameras trying to kick in the precinct's front door. That didn't deliver, so he then attacked the big glass door with large rocks, an act frowned upon by police departments, even in Florida. When officers took his arrest statement, the 50-year-old man said he was being chased by 20-25 people, which again, if you've spent time in Florida is, well, you know.

Maybe he was being harassed by the same German shepherds. Maybe in Orlando there was a convention.

Another guy tried to get in to the same police station by climbing over its 10-foot-high security fence (maybe he'd heard about that stubborn glass door). While on the fence, however, the break-in entrepreneur got impaled through the buttocks, which is unfortunate, unless you're writing a humor column.

But the best one (remember, we're still in Fort Lauderdale here) is this one: a naked man was arrested after running through a Florida neighborhood (again, not so odd, it's Florida – wait for it) and attempting to have sex with a tree (*there* it is). When the officers nabbed him while desperately trying to avert their eyes, the pesky little timber rattler told the police that he was the mythical god Thor.

Yep. The man tried to do the Humpty Dance with a hardy perennial, and then he said, "I'm Thor."

Or maybe he had a lisp.

One might be tempted to blame the city. Maybe it's just Fort Lauderdale. After all, this is a place invaded every spring by thousands of eventually naked college students who have driven hundreds of miles to work on their minor: mud-cage-wrestling while binge drinking. But authorities think the culprit is chemical: a new designer drug known as *flakka*, which is Spanish slang for *thin, pretty woman*. (Editor's note: the Spanish antonym for *flakka* is *Bruce Jenner*.)

But when it comes to drugs, don't think humans are having all the fun. In Utah, where lawmakers are voting to legalize medical marijuana, there's a growing concern that rabbits have developed a taste for pot and are getting an attitude. This very un-bunny-like behavior was noted by a member of the Drug Enforcement Agency's "cannabis eradication" team during a recent raid on an illegal marijuana patch in Utah.

"One of [the rabbits] refused to leave us, and we took all the marijuana around him, but his natural instincts to run were somehow gone," testified the special agent, who will remain nameless due to her or his seemingly helpless tendency to say stupid stuff.

So stick with it, NASA. Get that warp engine running, 'cause we're running out of time.

~-~-~-~-~-~-~-~-~-~-~

This just in: Utah's Great Salt Lake has been surrounded by very slow-moving bunny rabbits with glazed eyes and chocolate-chip cookie crumbs in their whiskers. The rogue rabbits, all sporting tie-dyed bandannas and humming reggae tunes, arrived in a caravan of electric vehicles and a cloud of patchouli. As of yet, the fierce mammals have made no demands, other than some more cookies, but many Utahans are refusing to leave their homes, possibly recalling a traumatic scene involving a feral rabbit from the movie *Monty Python and the Holy Grail.*

Future Chicken

Cosmic yawns, Korean studs, fragile frogs. Just another week.

<><><>~~~~~~~~~~~~~~~~~~~~~~~~~<><><>

Here are some actual headlines. Well, to a point. As Garrison Keillor once said (and I paraphrase): Truth, for a storyteller, is a good place to start. But truth won't get you all the way home.

~-~-~-~-~-~-~-~-~-~-~

NEW POLL: 3% THINK U.S. CONFLICT WITH ISIS GOING "VERY WELL"

According to a recent poll conducted by two high school sophomores, the majority of Americans think we are losing ground in the global war on terrorism, while three percent of those polled think we're doing great. Eleven percent think we should send in more Amazon.com drones, five percent asked if Jennifer Anniston is really pregnant, and six people thought ISIS was the name of a flower.

The pollsters admit, however, that with this polling sample there may be a larger than normal margin of error because they forgot about their "opinion poll" homework assignment until

127

Thursday, so at the last minute they had to interview a bunch of off-duty used car salesmen sitting at the bar in Hooter's. Two of the salesmen asked for ISIS' phone number.

SHORT KOREAN GUY CLIMBS 9,000-FOOT MOUNTAIN USING JUST ONE LEG

There's more amazing news out of North Korea about the amazing feats of Kim Jong-un, the only world leader in history to have a man-crush on Dennis Rodman.

According to sanctioned reports filed by the country's official newspaper (*The Great Happy World of Kim Daily News*), North Korea's diminutive leader...the man with the Chia-pet hairdo...has scaled Mount Paektu, the country's highest mountain. And based on the official photographs, he made the ascent wearing a topcoat and dress shoes.

This accomplishment comes as no surprise, of course: local legend portrays Kim as a supernatural being who by age three was already driving a car, scored 11 holes-in-one the very first time he played golf, and aced his college entrance exams while still *in utero*.

U.S. DEBT CONTINUES TO GROW; MATHEMATICIANS FORCED TO CREATE NEW NUMBER

After the administration's latest spate of Chinese borrowing, which is needed to fund Obama's new voter registration scheme -- direct distribution of food stamps to everybody in South America -- the United States debt now has so many

---

trailing zeroes that it's exceeded the accepted nomenclature used by world mathematicians...billion, trillion, gazillion just can't keep up.

At a hastily convened world summit of Grossly Incomprehensible Math Professors (GIMPs), it was suggested the "next number" be known as the *Fool-on-the-Hillion*, in honor of the U.S. Congress that keeps allowing this irrational thing to happen to rational numbers. (the GIMPs rejected a more pedestrian next number nomination, known as the *buttload*)

In related news, China has tendered a cash offer to buy Colorado, Montana, both Carolinas, and New Orleans.

HILLARY SHRUGS OFF FELONIES, CLAIMS PESKY LAWS AN 'INCONVENIENCE'

Today, on NBC News' completely non-partisan morning news show, *It's Hillary's Time!*, Sir Edmund Hillary Rodham Clinton, that Puerto Rican Jew from New York whose four grandparents were all Sicilian immigrants from Turkey, pinky-swore that every one of the 30,000 emails in question were personal in nature, not State Department-related, and that there's not a "shred of evidence" proving any wrongdoing, particularly since she shredded all 30,000 emails.

This makes candidate Clinton the first Presidential contender this election season to use "shred" as both a noun *and* a verb.

JOHN HOPKINS STUDENT GOVT BANS CHICK-FIL-A

Citing fears of theoretical "microagression" against the LGBTQ+ community, the student government association at prestigious Johns Hopkins University has voted to preemptively ban Chick-fil-A franchises from the campus, fearing the franchise's very presence would subject supporters of non-traditional marriage to a violent onslaught of gay-hating waffle fries.

Opponents of the SGA's pronouncement pointed out that there was not even a *plan* to build a Chick-fil-A at Johns Hopkins, so what the doomsayers were, um, doomsaying was effectively an irrational act based on fear of hypothetical chickens.

In a related story, the university has reversed a ban that would have prevented a pro-life group's anti-abortion display at the school's Spring Fair. Initially, the university had claimed that the group's display of the human fetus contained "triggering and disturbing images." Shortly thereafter, though, the massive irony underlying a medical school calling the human fetus "disturbing" was pointed out by about twenty billion people on Twitter.

SCIENTISTS DISCOVER REALLY BIG EMPTY PLACE

If you can believe CNN, which is entirely up to you, scientists have confirmed the existence of a "supervoid" in space, an awfully huge hole of nothing to see, much like Cleveland. The area is so large that it would take you 1.8 billion light-years to get from one side to the other, or even longer if you stopped for strict Protestant waffle fries or some future chicken.

The confirmation seems to back up much of current thought in the world of physics, claims an unnamed British scientist. "The universe does seem to work the way our model says it does," the scientist told CNN.

We didn't actually *see* the model's astrophysical credentials, but she was really cute.

OBAMA OBSERVES EARTH DAY, POISONS EVERGLADES

The President commemorated Earth Day by flying Air Force One (and two dozen support planes) into the Florida Everglades, just in case Florida ever secedes and needs an air force.

According to the White House, while in Florida the President "delivered remarks on the threat that climate change and our carbon footprint poses to the world." When asked if Air Force One releasing nearly 200,000 pounds of CO_2 into the atmosphere would contribute to the dreaded footprint, the White House made some huffy remark about George Bush.

Washington insiders point out that Democratic presidents always make a big show on Earth Day; during the Clinton presidency, as a massive motorcade went barreling through the pristine New England forests, one of the vehicles permanently flattened a beaver.

Later that day, Clinton "did not have sex" with the driver and he pardoned the beaver.

NY STATE JUDGE GRANTS HABEAS CORPUS TO TWO CHIMPS

For the first time ever, a judge on Long Island appears to have recognized two research lab chimpanzees as legal persons, granting them their day in court, and the right to challenge their detention, unless the chimps get caught bartering cartons of cigarettes.

There was some initial concern about the defense's ability to empanel a twelve-member jury, but the bailiff pointed out that the United Nations was nearby and the place is positively dripping with chimpanzee peers.

Celebrity attorney Gloria Allred offered to take the apes' case, but the chimps are holding out for an attorney with more scruples, or at least opposable thumbs.

NEWLY DISCOVERED FROG BEARS STRIKING RESEMBLANCE TO PRESIDENTIAL HOPEFULS

A scientist in Costa Rica is excited, perhaps justifiably, though we doubt it, for having discovered a new species of glass frog, news which may have excited other people, too, though we doubt it. The scientist has named the new frog *Hyalinobatrachium dianae*, because "Eddie" was already taken.

The glass frog is an extremely delicate egg-laying creature, like many politicians. It's so translucent that its internal organs are visible, but you gotta stand in a really uncomfortable position to see them...not to mention what the *frog* must be thinking. Politicians insist that, after a while, you get used to it.

This just in: upon hearing of the American voter's fascination with transparency, the frog has formed a presidential exploratory committee.

Barry Parham

America's Least Wanted

It's people like this who give crime a bad name

<><><>~~~~~~~~~~~~~~~~~~~~~~~~~~~<><><>

Criminals. Let's face it: when we think about the great ones – Al Capone, Pretty Boy Floyd, Bonnie & Clyde, Congress – *publicly*, we all tut-tut such bad behavior, but privately? We can't get enough. Well, except for Congress.

This month, the FBI's Ten Most Wanted List turns 65. Imagine that: for sixty-five years, millions of Americans have been studiously ignoring the ten surly mug shots in that famous document that we've all seen, usually when buying stamps. (It says a lot about the US Postal Service that when the Post Office designers got to the "tasteful décor" phase, the Most Wanted List is what they came up with. That, and air-brushed pictures of an eagle holding stamps.)

During those six-plus decades, over 500 bad guys (and a few bad girls) have made it to the Most Wanted list. In fact, only seven of the Most Wanteds were women, but I don't think that's due to some vague lack of career enthusiasm. Remember, the List is comprised of *uncaught* criminals, and based on my vast dating experience, women don't flee.

135

There's also a Top *Fifteen* Most Wanted list maintained by the U.S. Marshals Service, starring Tommy Lee Jones. As of this month, though, five of the fifteen bad guys (and they're all guys) have been captured, and another one, perhaps consumed with envy at not making the FBI list, died.

The guy most recently topping the Marshals' list was a self-proclaimed pastor from Pine City, Minnesota, which is in Pine County, Minnesota, proving that Minnesotans have serious creativity issues. The pastor was wanted for nearly sixty counts of criminal sexual assault, proving that Minnesota has Catholic priests. The unholy scoundrel was finally nabbed in Brazil, where he had been hiking the Appalachian trail with former South Carolina governor Mark Sanford.

And then there are the also-rans. The little criminals. The small-town small-time crooks. Sure, they dream of Most Wanted Lists; sure, they have felonious aspirations; sure, they had method, motive, and opportunity.

But they're also stupid.

Here are some of the more pedestrian villains of late, a list we lifted from various local police blotters:

- A thirty-nine-year-old man was detained after calling 911 to report that his wife stole his cocaine. The dispatcher told him to hang up and call Judge Judy.
- A man from the town of Brooksville was arrested for hitting a dog with a basketball. The suspect copped a

plea of temporary March Madness, according to his defense attorney, Michael Vick.

- Authorities say an Orlando man who robbed someone of their phone apparently panicked during the getaway and shot himself. He was arrested a short time later when he flagged down a deputy to ask for help. Then he filed a citizen's arrest against himself for shooting himself. The attending officer, realizing the amount of paperwork he'd have to fill out, just grabbed the thief and tossed him into the bed of a passing pick-up truck, piloted by a large Everglades alligator and an abandoned Burmese python who were heading to Disney World for their honeymoon. Nearing the theme park, the trio stopped for a bite at a Waffle House, where they were seated at a booth next to a horde of smartphone salesmen in town for a "productivity app" convention. The salesmen then pestered the thief about changing his calling plan until eventually he shot himself again.

- When questioned by police, a Palm Beach woman said the reason she sat naked outside a Dunkin' Donuts was because of a dare. And having heard this, may I make an earnest personal plea to every American: never dare Hillary Clinton.

- A Georgia man was arrested for drunk driving after he told deputies his dog drove him to the store to buy some corn. Despite the charges, the man intends to complete his term in the Georgia legislature; the dog, however, will have to surrender its driver's license and EBT card.

- A woman in Manatee, Florida, was arrested after she allegedly punched her sister in the face during an argument about a vibrator. (A vibrator, for those of you who don't get HBO, is a battery-powered device intended to replace a man, but without all the sports channels and beer.) When the police arrived, the marital aid-packing perp was observed on the victim's balcony, screaming obscenities. (An obscenity, for those of you who never heard Joe Biden, is an impolite word or phrase that you're not supposed to say, according to world-renowned sensitivity expert, George Carlin.) An on-the-scene reporter said the vibratee victim was not seriously injured, fortunately. The vibrator could not be reached for comment, also fortunately. And as a humorist, I could never look myself in the face again if I didn't throw in the fact that the vibrator-wielding suspect was officially charged with ... battery.

- Somewhere in Maine, a thirty-seven year old female was pulled over while wearing a Hello Kitty costume. She was eventually charged with DUI, and with impersonating an extremely lame Japanese line drawing.

- In western Pennsylvania, a tractor-trailer driver led police on a thirty-four mile chase, during which he threw stuff out of the cab window at the pursuing officers. The "stuff" included socks, shoes, and a small refrigerator. According to a news wire report, the jettisoned fridge contained a bag of jelly donuts, so all charges have been dropped.

- A man in Cedar Grove, New Jersey, was found passed out in a car wearing an elf costume (the man, not the car). The arresting officers were a bit dubious about the elf's explanation: that he was simply resting midway through his road trip to Maine to attend the wedding of the Hello Kitty lady.

- A naked citizen of Arab, Alabama, climbed a tree and has refused to come down, telling anyone who wandered by, happened to look up, and thought to ask, that he just planned to live there, in the tree. (Editor's note: according to the official website of Arab, Alabama, one of the town's cottage industries is basket-weaving. Somebody needs to weave a really big one.)

So, Happy 65th Birthday, Most Wanted List! Thank you for helping keep our communities safe from the bad guys.

As far the bad girls, I guess we're on our own.

Barry Parham

Guardians of the Guy Galaxy

Somebody's gotta do it.

Here at the American Institute for the Preservation of Guys and Other Endangered Species, we're always on the lookout for new hazards. We have to be; after all, we work for an organization whose mission is to try and protect guys – a moderately challenged life form consisting of upright bipeds (more-or-less) whose last words, all too often, are "Hey y'all - watch this!"

It's a thankless job, working for the Institute, especially during our quarterly motivational seminars, like *You & Your Colon*, and *Flossing Can Be Fun!* But it can also be an interesting job, particularly during Sodium Pentothal Week.

But thankless or not, it must be done. Left unattended, guys might "oops" themselves right out of existence. Remember: your average guy's idea of a good idea is to put on shorts in mid-winter and jump out of second-story windows, where snow will either break his fall or frozen landscaping will break his head.

And despite doing things like giggling at flatulence, or drinking beer through a funnel, guys are necessary to the human race, at least so far. Here's how much humanity depends on guys:

- They have half the stuff necessary to make more humans
- They are very easily amused, so they can adapt to domestication and they're not in the way all that much
- They take out the trash

So you can see why there's a need to protect guys. The very preservation of our species is dependent on the existence of guys, although it's true that, thanks to miraculous breakthroughs in reproductive theory and medical science, we are very close to a day when women will be able to take out the trash. And once guys lose *that* edge, there'll be nothing to stop women scientists from creating procreation androids that all look like David Tennant or Brad Pitt. Of course, that will inevitably lead to the election of a female President, who will extend the food stamp program to include shoes.

After that, for guys, it'll simply be a matter of "Hop on this ice floe, would you, dear?" as we're jettisoned to the seas, propelled into oblivion by a quick push from a tasteful pair of government-subsidized open-toed pumps.

But until then, our Institute will continue our efforts to shepherd guys through the shoals of guy life, and this week we'd like to touch on the topic of jobs – specifically, *losing* jobs. Getting fired. Recently, you see, we were made aware of an online article titled *Seven Signs You Will Be Fired Soon*. We looked over the article, and we have to admit that we haven't seen such a pile of useless drivel since Barack Obama sent Joe Biden out to all 57 States to spell the word "JOB" with four letters.

Here are some examples of the "advice" offered in the *Seven Signs* piece:

- You're no longer in the loop
- You don't get along with your boss
- You make a colossal mistake

Ah. Well. Isn't *that* handy! So ... everybody ignores you, your boss hates you, and your incompetence has reached a level that requires a thesaurus. Analysis? The clever crew at *Seven Signs* calculates that your job might be in jeopardy.

Hey, *Seven Signs*. Here's another professional tip: if your feet are wet, look down and see if there's water.

And so, for all you guys out there holding down a four-letter J-O-B, wondering if you're close to the hatchet, here are some real-world, actually *helpful* clues to tip you off that you might be near to getting a personalized pink slip:

How To *Really* Tell You're About To Be Fired

- Some clown tapes a sign to your chair that says *Employees Only*
- That cute girl in Accounting who would never go out with you because "dating, like, co-workers and stuff is like totally not a good idea" suddenly invites you to Vermont

- You get an email from Human Resources that contains the phrase "final warning."
- Recently, your supervisor has begun referring to you as "Whaddaycallit"
- Somebody keeps taking your lunch out of the fridge and putting it in the *Help the Down & Out* donation box
- The guys in IT re-route your office extension to a street-side phone booth
- The head of your department walks around the building introducing everybody to some mousey bespectacled teen: "This is Millie, my wife's sister's niece. She just graduated!" And what Millie just graduated *in* is what *you* do.
- Human Resources sends you a memo that is "just a friendly reminder" to double-check your beneficiaries and next of kin
- You walk in one morning and everyone on your team is running about, darting in and out of your cubicle, grabbing and waving your stuff and shouting "Dibs!"

So, stay sharp, guys. Know the signs, keep a low profile, and take out the trash. You can do this. You've made it through vastly more confusing things, like puberty and other events that involved too much guilt, too little Scotch-Guard, and no instructions whatsoever.

Remember – the Institute for the Preservation of Guys has got your back.

B-A-K.

Equally Cold Calls

Sometimes you have to bite the dog back.

Ever get an unsolicited telemarketing call and decide to just run with it? You should. It's free, it's good for you, and it has zero trans-fat.

Besides, toying with telemarketers is one of your guaranteed Constitutional rights, enumerated right there between your right to have a seizure and your right to not have your bare arms searched.

And ... they asked for it. After all:

- *they* called *you*
- it's legal for telemarketers to lie to *you*, so lying to *them* is pretty much open season
- technically speaking, telemarketers aren't from this planet

To be fair, it's (usually) not the telemarketers' fault, especially that last point about being aliens. Telemarketing is just a job like any other job, except for the part where everybody you

145

speak to hates you. Cold-calling people all day every day is a hard life. I know. I've done it.

In the mid-80s, as part of my post-university career plan – my plan was to retire *first*, then maybe settle into a career later, what's the big rush -- I packed my six personal possessions (two shirts, two pairs of jeans, a pair of shoes and a music player) and moved from Southern California to North Miami. When I arrived in South Florida, however, I discovered that Miami had officially defected to Cuba, and no bar or lounge in the land would hire a bartender who didn't know how to *habla*.

I had to find a job, and quickly. And since I wasn't qualified for your normal South Florida entry-level jobs – I didn't have the seed money to invest in a starter bale of marijuana, and I didn't know how to say, in Spanish, "Hi, my name's Barry and I'm available to be your international cocaine mule" – I took a job as a telemarketer.

Five days a week, we would huddle in oddly-stained cubes with mountains of thermal-printed lists inside windowless rooms that always smelled of pork and plantains, and for hour after hour we would cold-call car dealerships with names like Tulsa Dodge World (*"Home of the Steel Wheel Real Deal!"*) and Big Tiny's One-Owner Used-Auto Graveyard. (*"Where High Prices Go To Die!"*)

And our plum job was to sell radio ads to these caffeine-crazed, margin-guarding, bolo-tie-wearing deal-dancers.

Winding Down Civilization

It was a mad, maddening, Gatling-gun-paced whipsaw of a ride that drove me so insane I ended up getting engaged. But let's not pick at *that* thread. Not today.

Needless to say, I didn't stick around long enough to sweat and claw my way to a leadership position in the coveted inner circle of North Miami Nondescript Strip Mall-Based Outbound Call Center Boiler Room middle management. Oh, el *heck*, no.

So now I'm just a simple single guy who got a cold call, and decided to run with it.

And when I say "run with it," I don't just mean simply re-running one of the anti-cold-call classics, like pretending you only speak a foreign language, or asking them to hold for a second while you put the phone on the counter, lock your house, go have your car detailed, catch a movie, get that nose job you've been putting off, and then drive to the grocers with your full monthly shopping list.

I'm talking about a full-on, fangs-drawn but still low-key hostility. I'm talking about a focused, dedicated, short-term confrontational relationship, one that demands equal doses of spicy subtlety, rich, lightning-fast ripostes, and a dash of hob-nailed boots.

And it's not often I make a commitment.

[*ring*]

Me: This is Barry.

Leaf-Slayer: Hi. This is Mumbled Name calling from Leaf-Slayer. Is this James Parham?

Me: Yes.

Leaf-Slayer: Here at Leaf-Slayer, our motto is "We H8 Leaves!" Isn't that clever!

Me: Yes, you should all be very proud.

Leaf-Slayer: See how we spelled *hate* with an "8" there?

Me: Lady, this is a *phone call*. I can't see how you spelled "hate."

Leaf-Slayer: What?

Me: Good word, though, "hate." I'm contempl8ting it this very minute.

Leaf-Slayer: Is this James Parham?

Me: Yes, still. What was your name again?

Leaf-Slayer: Mumbled Name.

Me: Hi, Missus Name. Or can I call you Mumbled?

Leaf-Slayer: We've been trying to reach you about an estimate.

Me: No, thank you.

Leaf-Slayer: Is this James Parham?

Me: Yes, darling. It *is* "darling," isn't it?

Leaf-Slayer: We've been trying to reach you about an estimate.

Me: I know how you feel. I've been trying to ignore you trying to reach me about an estimate.

Leaf-Slayer: Is this James?

Me: Yes, you persistent, hot thing. It's still me. Hey, I'm gonna go out on a limb here and ask: you called for a reason?

Leaf-Slayer: We've been trying to reach you about an estimate.

Me: No, thank you. Good-bye.

Leaf-Slayer: You've picked another solution?

Me: No. Good-bye.

Leaf-Slayer: What?

Me: Good-bye. "Good-bye." It's a fairly common word except, apparently, in telemarketing circles, and other primitive cultures. Look it up.

Leaf-Slayer: What?

Me: Sorry. Google it.

Leaf-Slayer: You've picked another solution?

Me: No.

Leaf-Slayer: What?

Me: What are you wearing?

Leaf-Slayer: Is this James?

Me: Hold on, I'll check my camp underwear.

Leaf-Slayer: What?

Me: Yes, it's me. Assuming I can read my Mom's handwriting.

Leaf-Slayer: What?

Me: Look, I don't need my foliage slain.

Leaf-Slayer: I understand your hesitation. What are you using now for vital, life-enhancing gutter management?

Me: It's complicated.

Leaf-Slayer: What?

Me: From August till November, I sit on my roof and slap leaves out of my gutters with a jaded ferret who read too much Sylvia Plath. Unless, of course, it's a day when my Druid cult is meeting.

Leaf-Slayer: Is this James?

Me: No, is this?

Leaf-Slayer: What?

Barry Parham

Ennui-Gate

It may not be interesting, but it sure is boring.

<><><>~~~~~~~~~~~~~~~~~~~~~~~<><><>

Last week, several chunks of the Earth blew up and floated into space. And lo, there was great wailing and gnashing of teeth over the loss, except for the California chunk. (Detroit was also atomized by an alien spaceship's death ray, but city planners admitted the new look was actually an improvement.)

Last week, all disease was eradicated from the face of the planet, mankind discovered a solution for world hunger, and the federal government of the United States stopped collecting taxes after confessing they really had all the money they needed for bridges and stuff.

There were various other miracles that occurred last week, too, like an entire six month period without the release of a new iPhone, and for three consecutive minutes, nobody in the White House lied.

None of that actually happened, of course...especially the bit about the White House. But it might have happened -- and we'd have never known. Why? What riveting Earth-shaker of a story hijacked the headlines?

Limp footballs.

In case you aren't following the story -- or in case President Obama confiscated your TV to give it to someone who doesn't have as many as you -- here's a recap: after the Indianapolis Colts got gang-spanked in a pre-Super Bowl playoff, they accused the victorious New England Patriots of...now stay with me here...tinkering with the game balls.

I think you'll agree that no forward-looking civilization can allow this kind of madness to continue.

Apparently, the National Football League has inviolate rules governing how much air any given football has to have. (These are the same social guardians who think it's a capital offense for a player to celebrate in the end zone after scoring a touchdown. Dancing is *Not Allowed*. Maybe the NFL rules committee are Baptists.) However, according to about 57 million post-game reports and news conferences, eleven of the Patriots' twelve game balls were discovered to be "underinflated significantly below the league requirements."

The upshot of this vile crime spree is that the Patriots' quarterback (Tom Brady) and their head coach (young Marcia Brady) are now suspected of pigskin tampering -- and they're both delivering pretty fair impersonations of Sergeant Schultz from *Hogan's Heroes*. They. Know. Nothing.

The under-inflated football was discovered after one of the Colts' defensive mutants intercepted one of Brady's passes, stared accusingly at the ball, and remarked, "You know, I question whether this football is properly inflated to between 12.5 and 13.5 pounds per square inch, even though it was tested by the referee two hours and fifteen minutes before kickoff as our sacred rules require." Then he headed for the sidelines, where he playfully bit a cameraman, sucker-punched a couple of Patriot cheerleaders, and plopped down on the bench to finish his raw meat sandwich.

Next, as you might imagine, the media went bat-stark insane. "Deflate-gate," they christened the travesty. According to one heavily-hair-gelled plaid-sports-jacket-sporting sports analyst, the event has "turned into a full-fledged national scandal that's transcended sports."

Ooh. Ooh. Contain your emotions. *Something has transcended sports.*

Hey, Hair Gel. My *elbow* transcends sports.

And the analysts will *not* let it go. Every TV channel is spiriting up its own inflation experts: equipment managers; NFL ball boys; Alan Greenspan; the Michelin Man.

(Did you know the Michelin Man has a name? The French named him *Bibendum*. Apparently, making tires in France can get furiously boring.)

Some quarterbacks say Tom Brady *has* to have done it...or known it. Nobody, they say, messes with a field general's balls, and I'm sorry but there's no way I could get through an entire humor column on a subject like this without at least one cheap "balls" joke. Let's hope I got it out of my system.

Other career sportscasters are blaming the coach. On the other hand, some air pressure pundits point out that it would be nearly impossible, due to league procedures and live TV coverage, to deflate game balls without being noticed -- much less to deflate eleven footballs to exactly two pounds under spec. What if the air pressure manipulator went too far and *over* deflated? Now he's on the sidelines during the biggest game of the season, in view of every network TV camera in the Northern Hemisphere, schlepping around with a bicycle air pump.

"Hey, kid! What are you doing with that air pump?"
"Uh...one of the cheerleaders lost a breast."
"You're doing the Lord's work, son."

However this dulling Deflate-gate debacle turns out, it's hardly the first scandal in the world of sports. In fact, this is not the first time the Patriots have been caught acting like a member of Congress during a tough re-election. In a 2007 game with the NY Jets, the Pats were accused of videotaping and decoding the Jets' sideline signals, which resulted in the Allies defeating Hitler (in overtime). And the (North) Carolina Panthers still think the Patriots pulled a fast one to secure a victory in Super Bowl XXVIII; however, we note that the Panthers' selectively-outraged spokespanther skated right past a published report that several players on the team had bought steroids from a South Carolina physician. (in South Carolina it's not illegal to transport under-aged pharmaceuticals across state lines)

Over the years, there've been lots more. Let's review a few:

- Lance Armstrong, seven-time Tour de France champion, admitted to using performance-enhancing drugs when he rode for the US Postal Service Pro-Cycling Team (and if ever anybody could use some performance-enhancing drugs, it's the US Postal Service). As part of his punishment, Sir Lance had to endure being interviewed by Oprah.

- Not long ago, Major League Baseball superstars like Mark McGwire, Sammy Sosa, and Barry Bonds confessed to taking steroids after a linesman noticed they were having to shave between innings. In one memorable game, a hyper-jittery Sosa hit a home run, fielded his own ball, and threw himself out.

- Cincinnati Reds catcher Pete Rose was once accused of betting on baseball games, including games the Reds had already lost. To this day, Pete is still refused consideration for the Major League Baseball Hall of Fame. But at least he didn't have to get interviewed by Oprah.

- More recently, former Penn State defensive coordinator Jerry Sandusky was indicted for illegally impersonating Pee Wee Herman.

- Let's hop back to 1994, for Olympics figure skating, that most violent of sports, when favorite Nancy Kerrigan was attacked by Tonya Harding and her husband (Warren G.), who both gracefully clubbed Nancy in the leg. Harding would go on to invent the sport of Roller Derby, a crowd-pleasing combination of rugby and NASCAR for pro-choice women with abdominal tattoos.

- Tiger Woods should've just let the year 2009 play through. In less time than it takes Dan Marino to negotiate with Nutrisystem, the PGA star got caught with more than a dozen mistresses, went through a divorce, checked in to therapy, and his ex-wife tried to kill his car.

- Three words: Howard Cosell's toupee. Scandal? Maybe not. Travesty? You make the call.

- Perhaps most infamous - baseball's "Black Sox" scandal, when eight members of the Chicago White Sox were banned from baseball for life for throwing the 1919 World Series, a shame made more shameful given Chicago's historical aversion to any kind of corruption.

- And what serious sports fan can forget sumo wrestling's notorious hazing scandal -- and of course we're talking about the Tokitsukaze Stable here -- in which a fraternity-like ritual between wrestler wannabees got out of hand, leaving one of the sumo pledges with a serious case of not being alive? It's a bitter pill, but this is the kind of senseless tragedy that can happen in a sport where oversized men in loincloths clutch. Perhaps if they'd only heard Dan Marino's spiel for Nutrisystem...

- Finally, as we close our little discussion of sports world scandals, let's give an honorable mention to OJ Simpson -- Heisman Trophy winner, ex-murder suspect, and now in prison for robbery. Take a note, kids. That "never give up" mindset is all too rare today.

~-~-~-~-~-~-~-~-~-~-~

So...

New England Patriots -- good luck in the Super Bowl.

And to *both* teams: if you can drag out the game ... by any means whatsoever: by soul-kissing the game balls; by accusing Tom Brady of kidnapping the Lindbergh baby; by taking an official timeout to air a film of John Madden's colon polyps; whatever ... Do it!

Because as soon as the Super Bowl is over, every sports fan knows what horror awaits:

League Bowling.

Barry Parham

Liberté, Egalité, Tuna Fish

How Napoleon saved kitchen gadgets

<><><>~~~~~~~~~~~~~~~~~~~~~~~~~<><><>

Here's a tip from the instructions that came with my new electric can opener:

Do not place in a heated oven.

And thus, another life was saved. Because I was *this* close...

Since the day after the dawn of time, humankind has looked at food and wondered, "How can I store this for later, when it's cold out?" And while humankind was working it out, there were always a few guys over in the corner, eyeballing various objects and thinking, "You know what'd be cool? Throw it in the fire."

Fortunately, however, humankind has managed to survive, despite the antics of untamed guys, thanks to an invention known as the *remote control*, a rectangular mind management device that can keep your average guy entertained for days.

161

As you've probably grasped by now unless you're an idiot with an oven, I finally had to replace my old can opener, which I've had since, roughly, Vietnam. Year after year, it just quietly sat there not multitasking on the counter, faithfully opening cans of corn, or tuna, or repurposed chemicals for the meth lab. Then, last week, after positioning a can and stabbing it with the can opener's medieval metal plunger, nothing happened. Silence. The motor had stopped moting. The can didn't smoothly spin, the top didn't politely separate. My sensible response, of course, was to apply guy diagnostics -- I slapped the thing's level up and down. I slapped it several times. I also tried to encourage it verbally. But I was too late. The can opener was a goner. What's worse - it was nearly lunchtime and here I was, stuck holding a dysfunctional tin of tuna with an air hole punched in its lid.

My new electric can opener came with twenty pages of operating instructions, helpful tips, and dire warnings, all presented in English, Spanish, and French. Thanks to the manual, I now know how to say "the motor is permanently lubricated" in Spanish; you know, should it ever come up during border negotiations, or late night in some South American prison. (Interestingly, all the French warnings ended the same: *In the event of [insert can opener problem here], run away.*)

As you might imagine, can opener technology has come a long way since the days of Richard Nixon, not that there's any direct link between the two that you could prove without independent counsel, or access to the tapes, or a deeply throated source. My amazing new kitchen timesaver works, not by cutting through the lid, but by separating the entire top from the can ... kind of a Marie Antoinette approach to getting at the groceries.

My recently deceased can opener followed a model more reminiscent of the Spanish Inquisition. To get what it wanted out of a can, my ex-can opener would force a blunt metal blade through the can's equally metal top, then relentlessly rotate the captive, gouging its way around the circumference, suturing the steel until it jettisoned, at which point the water-packed tuna would finally confess to being a witch.

Here's another warning from the kindler gentler can opener's instructions:

Do not hold the can while the can is being opened.

This advice, I suppose, is intended to reduce your chances of rapidly going round in circles, which could cause an observer to confuse you with the US Congress.

And another:

Hold lever down for one rotation only. Allowing only one rotation reduces or prevents metal slivers.

What? *Metal slivers?* And what do you mean, *reduces?*

Man, I bet the pressure boys at the Spanish Inquisition home office would love to get their hands on this thing.

Maybe I'm over-reacting. For all I know, I've been tucking in to tuna laced with metal slivers my whole old-school-can-

163

opener life. After all, the "shove sharp metal into metal and carve" can-opening technique has been around since Napoleon, and yet we've seen very few verifiable reports of people getting mangled by tomato soup or pointy tuna, even among guys.

Can Opener Historical Footnote: The reason we have can openers is because we have cans (*source: Joe Biden*). And the reason we have cans is thanks to Napoleon Bonaparte, a short, edgy French guy who compensated for his height issues by invading various European countries while wearing a hat shaped like a pool ball rack.

In 1795, Napoleon offered a reward to anyone who could develop a safe way to preserve food for his army, a ragtag group known as the French Foreign Lesion. (fight song: *Let's geaux! Let's geaux! Then geaux and geaux some meaux!*) It took fifteen years for the winner, Nicholas Appert, to invent the world's first airtight can, but nobody had invented the can opener yet, so Napoleon's army died anyway.

In 1858, the popular Mason Jar was introduced (named after its creator, John Jar). Unfortunately, the product line had to be recalled after some idiot guy stuck a case of them in a heated oven.

Of course, most cans these days have a pop-top, making electric can openers less relevant to all but the dumbest guys, and members of Congress. Either way, though, I'm set. According to the instructions, my brand new can opener can behead both the old-school cans *and* the newer, kindler, gentler pop-top varietals.

And with minimal metal slivers!

Barry Parham

Don't Forget To Tip Your Server-Person!

America: every woman a king

If you look around at some of America's trends and statistics ... if you observe the types of things people consider important these days ... you might be tempted to pack it in and relocate to a foreign country, like Ireland, or California. But for the soldiers (and soldierettes) in our ongoing campaign to de-genderfy America, it's been a good year.

So there's that.

Here's an example: A guy who owns an Italian restaurant in the Big Apple is in trouble -- as in *five thousand dollar fine* trouble -- because he advertised on Craig's List for ... ready? ... a waitress and a hostess.

Gasp. The toad! He deserves the chair.

Apparently, it's now some psychotic form of sexual discrimination to say "waitress" in New York City. It seems some local whiners from the Human Rights Commission have mandated that the man (can we say "man?") use the more politically correct, gender-neutral terms "host" and "server," and I wish these meddling irritants would "shut up."

On the other hand, we might want to keep an eye on this guy; after all, he *does* hang out on Craig's List.

Meanwhile, on the other coast: at a high school in Huntington Beach, a boy beat out nine other contestants and was crowned Homecoming Queen. In a tearful follow-up interview, his or her highness said that she or he had always felt like a girl, a comment uttered many times by Wilt Chamberlain, and Bill Clinton. So the Homecoming nee King is "making the transition" to living as a girl (she's already acquired an impressive collection of open-toed shoes). Additionally, the child has been taking hormone blockers and receiving estrogen injections, so his or her parents must've moved to Ireland.

(By the way -- the high school's football team is known as the Vikings, which isn't really relevant to this story, but if you think I'm gonna let that ironic little detail go unsaid, you don't know much.)

And now we're getting hit in the face with the news about an Olympic gold medal-collecting swimmer and his "self-proclaimed" girlfriend, who used to be a boyfriend. The "self-proclaimed" girlfriend, now named Taylor, was born a David. But while the athlete was cross-training, David was cross-dressing. The swimmer signed on with Team USA; Dave went free agent.

(For the innocents out there -- what *self-proclaimed girlfriend* means, technically, is *not his girlfriend*. This is the kind of *self-serving bilge* you often hear from *publicity-hunting liars*.)

And like our evolving friend in Huntington Beach, Taylor/Dave decided to live like a girl, take testosterone blockers, and participate in a disciplined makeover that included corrective surgery and endless hours watching *The Lifetime Channel*.

Actually, it turns out that the Olympic swimmer's freestyle friend was born with *two* sexes, which seems awfully unfair to people like Jabba the Hutt and Hillary Clinton, who have none.

(For the innocents out there -- that "two sexes" thing is a rare condition known as *intersex*, the politically correct term preferred over the phrase we used to use: *Woody Allen*. You rarely see an intersex person, because, well, because they're rare. But they also don't get out much ... the male side is grumpy because he hates his job and his wife takes *forever* to get dressed, and the female half has an abnormal fear of gluten.)

And so it goes. People everywhere, thinking they can switch genders by swapping clothes, or names, or naughty bits. Enhancements, removals, reversals, implants, deplants. Welcome to America - where any boy can grow up to be a girl.

Look, you can put a dishwasher in a kennel, but that doesn't make it a beagle.

But in case you're still gender-shopping, here's a few lists with several options, from a website dedicated to hooking up people who are into bondage. Yes, there is such a website. And no, we won't include all the choices ... this website has more orientation options than a Ryan's lunch buffet, but with less sneeze guards.

(For the innocents out there -- *bondage* means intentionally inflicting pain on your partner immediately, rather than spreading it out over several years.)

Ready? Let's get started!

Gender
- Male
- Female (we note that "Male" and "Female" top the list. Apparently, it's okay to use the M-word and the F-word when you're shopping for kinky.)
- Cross-dresser (we think this is just cheating. Where's the commitment? It's like sexual dysfunction lite.)
- Gender Fluid (we don't know what this means, but we wouldn't want to be the bathroom attendant)
- Butch (as opposed to Sundance)
- Femme (sounds French -- see *sexual dysfunction lite*)
- Not Applicable (now *that's* just plain lazy)

Sexual Orientation
- Straight (aka; dudes that like babes)
- Gay (aka; babes that like Fred Flintstone)
- Heteroflexible (aka; dudes that like Stretch Armstrong)
- Pansexual (aka; goat-lovers -- see *US Congress*)
- Fluctuating/Evolving (popular among current US Presidents)

- Asexual (then why are you visiting a bondage website?)
- Unsure (all right, who let the slow kid in?)

At the bondage website, there's also a section that lets you choose your "Role." You can select from dozens, including Dominant, Submissive, Daddy, Brat, Switch, Primal, and something called Kajira, which the website describes as a "female slave of Gor." So apparently that climate-crazed former Vice President got up to much more than just inventing the internet, eh?

And lastly, for that enquiring bondage novice, there's "Unsure." I guess you just show up at the clubhouse, bring a blindfold, and hang on.

Of course, some will say "to each his own." But it creeps. The American Re-genderifcation war creates casualties among the bystanders, too. People on the sidelines, like me. For example, I'm now getting spam from companies trying to sell me a bra. One of them even promises a product that will help control "side spillage."

I hate when that happens.

Barry Parham

Dr. Skippy & the Sun Gods

It must be legit - I saw it online.

The guy's credentials began like this:

"For more than four hundred million years, I have protected the borders between the physical world and the worlds of shadow."

So I knew I'd found a plumber I could trust.

I'm kidding, of course. It's *never* that easy to find a good plumber.

No, the above quip came from a consciousness-awakening website, one of the billions of resources out there that promise to connect you with the cosmos while separating you from your wallet. This particular guru - we'll call him Dr. Skippy - also claims to be a protector of this "infant race" the rest of us know as, well, *us*. Dr. Skippy warns that if weren't for the efforts of "his kind," mankind would be at the mercy of all sorts of extraterrestrial evil entities, as if the entire galaxy were filled with members of Congress.

("His kind." We've all met "his kind" before. These are the people you often see on the news, wearing loose-fitting clothing and highly-reflective hats, waiting for a comet to swing round and shuttle them back to the thin-fingered species-seeders on Neurotica Nine.)

So be thankful. Why, if not for Dr. Skippy, the Axis of Interplanetary Evil would "enslave, consume, and otherwise destroy the whole planet" -- though we think *and otherwise destroy* was a bit of a flourish. I mean, if the bad guys consume the planet, nobody's gonna be around for Act III and the *and otherwise destroy* scene.

But thanks, Dr. Skippy.

Fortunately for us mere mortals, Dr. Skippy has managed to condense all the secrets of the universe into his blog, where Dr. Skippy also hawks his self-help books:

- How to Find Your Spiritual Parents
- How to Find Your Spiritual Parents' Wallet
- Mastering the Gluten-Free Tao
- Applied Numerology (or *Why 7 8 9*)
- You Won't Go Blind

Yes. As evidenced by that last title, Dr. Skippy also thinks there are gods living in the sun, a discovery Dr. Skippy made during his college days, when he "used to stare at the sun for long periods of time."

(We're guessing that Dr. Skippy also used to put lots of non-controlled substances under his tongue and then shriek when his desk walked across the dorm room and ate a bat.)

Dr. Skippy insists that he's had first-hand encounters with ... um ... people who live inside the sun, and he can show you how to see them, too. And all without hallucinogenic drugs, Dr. Skippy quickly points out. (perhaps *too* quickly, if you get my drift)

Obviously, Dr. Skippy has advanced beyond simple bipededness. As further conclusive proof that you should buy his books, Dr. Skippy anecdotally relates that he once yelled "EXPELLIARMUS" at a dog, and the dog ran away.

Hard to argue with pure science.

"But books are, like, so sterile and stuff," you may be saying, but probably not, because you're texting. "When it comes to getting my chakra on and my karma on, I wanna, like, *involve* and stuff LOL."

Well, you have plenty of options to reach out and touch someone, preferably someone downwind. Take, for example, the recent karmic klatch known as the "Burning Man" Festival, an annual gathering of uninhibited free spirits who've moved beyond hide-bound, restrictive social conventions like fossil fuels, monogamy, and deodorant; a "transformative" affair in which people go to the desert, achieve transformative nakedness, and form a human crop circle. And apparently, Burning Man is catching on -- this year, they made the

Guinness Book of World Records as the only group of dusty naked morons visible from outer space.

For a few days each year, the Burning Maniacs stand around listening to music, making pithy observations, and occasionally wearing clothes, before returning home to their regular day jobs of annoying the spit out of the rest of us. This year's event proved particularly transformative, when the attendees all got attacked by Occupy Wall Street mosquitos and contracted the West Nile Virus.

And they say karma has no sense of humor.

Werewolves of New London

Why pets in New England always seem so edgy

<><><>~~~~~~~~~~~~~~~~~~~~~~~~~<><><>

This past week, thanks to a news piece out of New England, we were all treated to one of those storybook moments, like the time Dennis Rodman nearly married himself. You know the classic fairy tale formula: boy meets dog; boy falls for dog; boy sings naked; cops arrest boy; dog dies of shame.

Yet another timeless tale of unrequited love. But with a nice twist. Here's the headline out of Connecticut:

Naked Man Accused of Molesting Pit Bull in Neighbor's Yard, Says ISIS Sent Him

And they say *Virginia* is for lovers.

If you're like me, when the conversation turns to Extremely Weird Things I Read in the Paper, Connecticut is not exactly the Sodom that springs to mind. When I think of Connecticut, I think of milder, gentler phrases:

- Algonquin

177

- Mohicans
- Life insurance

On the other hand, don't forget that Connecticut is one of only two States that never ratified the 18th Amendment, the "Prohibition" law. (The other State was Saudi Arabia.) For several hundred years now in Connecticut, binge drinking has apparently been the order of the day, which may help explain some of Connecticut's historical antics. For example, on whatever night it was that their forefathers held the vote for Connecticut's State Animal -- and chose the sperm whale -- you just know tankards and grog were involved.

And one has to assume adult beverages played a part in this Connecticut news item about a guy who molested a pit bull and then blamed his prurient puppy pawing on a radical militia that's currently rezoning Iraq. Let's review some of the story's details, according to the reporter who filed the piece:

A woman in Waterbury CT claims she heard a "ruckus" in her back yard, where she kept a pit bull tethered to an 800-pound tow chain. (*Ruckus* is an old Algonquin term meaning *"indiscriminate sex with an entirely different species."*) And nobody could've been more surprised than her to discover that one of her neighbors was out there, although none of his clothes were, and the spunky fellow was doing some kind of sick Bill Clinton impersonation, except *this* intern was leashed to a Yukon-gauge logging chain and hadn't brought a pizza.

The aghast homeowner, who for whatever intensely personal reason was holding a citronella candle, threw it. As one might.

Then she yelled the four words that every homeowner hopes they will never have to yell:

"Get off my dog!"

This is beginning to get intense, so let's take a short break for a few more...

Fun Facts From Connecticut!

- In Hartford, Connecticut's capital, it is against the law the walk across the street on your hands. *(see "tankards and grog")*
- If only more States had refused to ratify Prohibition, Sean Connery wouldn't have had to die in *The Untouchables.*
- For much of its storied history, Connecticut was known the Constitution State, but they decided to ditch the "Constitution" nickname after a disoriented Barack Obama kept trying to trample on it.
- In 1878, America's first phone book was printed in New Haven, Connecticut, according to a website that calls itself Enchanted Learning with a straight face. In an unrelated story, people in colonial New Haven often used pumpkins as guides to ensure a nice, round, uniform haircut. Maybe they invented phone books to help locate a Supercuts.
- Fortunately for all of mankind, however, the "pig rodeo" craze was short-lived.

When Citronella Lady confronted her naked neighbor with the quite reasonable request to please stop doing the Humpty

Dance with her attack canine, he began "prancing" around the yard, claiming he was an agent of ISIS and yelling "This is our day and you have to prosper in it," a stunt not even Bill Clinton could pull off without a teleprompter.

The lady dashed back inside, called 911, and grabbed her gun, which we assume was a larger caliber sidearm than the candle. Then she realized that all her bullets were locked up inside her car's glove box, assumedly so she could scatter-gun her way through a turnpike toll booth, or in case she got car-jacked by an out-of-work pig-rodeo clown.

She displayed her weapon to the fashion-challenged lawn dancer, but as you can imagine, a naked man who's already been caught flirting with your dog doesn't scare easily. So she fired a warning shot into the ground, which is a tricky maneuver to pull off when all your ammo is still in the car.

Then, as the background music swelled and Alfred Hitchcock stepped in for his cameo, the denuded neighbor spread his arms and slowly staggered toward the woman with the still-warm weapon and the now-strained candle budget, as the dog smoked a cigarette.

And that's when the cops arrived. Two black-and-whites, fresh from quelling a bar fight between
ISIS militants who'd taken the wrong exit and unruly life insurance salesmen from Hartford. (*see "tankards and grog"*)

Naked Boy is now in custody and is undergoing a psychiatric evaluation. (*see "pumpkin-heads"*)

Yeah, we might want to keep an eye on this midnight dog-whisperer guy. He might do something crazy.

Barry Parham

Death By Niblick

Goat godfathers dispensing vigilante justice

Thanks to the news this week, we learned several things about ourselves:

- Nobody trusts the government
- Everybody's ready to give California back
- Somebody really hates chicken

On the other hand, we also learned a few things about our country:

- Nobody in the government trusts *us*, either. And that's probably smart. The way things are going, some of us are just about ready to start printing our own money.
- Maybe old-school phones didn't have apps and *Angry Birds*, but at least they didn't bend.
- No matter how bad things get in America, at least we don't have magic goats robbing banks.

First, let's get the goat business out of the way. According to a newspaper clipping posted online, police in Nigeria are holding a goat on suspicion of armed robbery.

It gets better. It's a shape-shifting goat.

Witnesses say armed robbers with extremely low aspirations were trying to steal a Mazda 323 when the heist went sour. The report went on to say -- and you'll have to trust me on this one -- "one [robber] escaped while the other turned into a goat."

After a fierce three-hour gunfight, the goat surrendered.

As it turns out, the mojo-enhanced goat had quite a rap sheet, and stealing ugly Japanese hatchbacks was just part of the picture. The goat was the kingpin of a nefarious international gang that kidnaps under-aged chickens and brainwashes them, which, if you've ever *met* a chicken, wouldn't take very long. The goat then sends the re-programmed pullets to California where they spend the rest of their lives voting for liberals.

And speaking of California: in a recent poll, 53% of Americans said they'd like to see California tossed out of the Union, preferably when the Union is moving at high speed in heavy traffic. To put this into some perspective, however, 25% of those polled felt we'd be better off without New York, and Texas came in a close third at 20%. (Another ten percent couldn't understand the question because it was in English, and forty-two people thought Detroit was a State.)

Now. Concerning that clutch of clowns in Washington DC that nobody trusts, where to begin?

- They publish official documents full of head-scratchers like this: "Photo ID is required to vote absentee in person."

- They refuse to let us harvest our own oil; meanwhile, we have to buy oil from overseas at hotel mini-bar prices.

- They've transformed the IRS into a Personal Vendetta Squad for the White House, an untouchable gang with the morals of a Joe Pesci character, except less endearing.

- Un-fire-able federal workers watch porn at work -- when they're not attending taxpayer-funded motivational seminars, where they're forced to watch porn from hotel rooms.

- Not only does the Secret Service get caught doing the Humpty Dance with hotel hookers in Colombia, they let a guy with a three-inch knife make it over the White House fence, across the lawn, past the alarms, down the hall and almost to the West Wing before they tackled the maniac and returned him to the Biden residence.

- Smarmy bureaucrats and pompous politicians pile-drive an obscenely flawed and intrusive Universal Health Care plan into law (without reading it) because -- so they claimed -- our health care system was in such bad shape. But then when people in Toe Ratchet, Idaho, start catching Ebola simply by standing too close to Liberia in a game of *Risk*, these same bureaucrats tell us not too worry because we have the best health care system on the planet.

185

- And then they beg for financial donations so they can get re-elected, go back to Washington, and fight for term limits.

But then, just to keep us regular folks humble, comes this story from ... you guessed it ... California. Here's the headline:

920 CHICKENS BEATEN TO DEATH WITH GOLF CLUB

I know. You'd think after about fifteen or so went down, the other 900 chickens would try to get out of the way.

Based on a report filed by the Fresno County Sheriff's Office, a suspect with some serious poultry issues snuck up on a local chicken processing plant, pulled back a portion of the perimeter fence, and entered the yard-bird yard with an alleged golf club.

The weapon appears to have been a nine iron, according to Burl Stoetagg, forensic pathologist for the Greater Fresno area, and yes, "greater Fresno" *is* its own joke. However, Burl was basing his findings on little more than a scorecard dropped by the suspects, divot analysis, and the fairway hang time of a badly shanked chicken part.

The assaulted chicken plant was immediately criticized for lax security, as though every other chicken dis-assembly facility in the US had assault contingency scenarios and henhouse evacuation plans. Firing back, the biddy bulk euthanasia palace quickly issued a PR statement to the media. "It is the express policy of this company to treat its birds humanely and with compassion," claimed Eula Dorritt, a company spokesperson, "right up to the part where we wring their necks and eat 'em."

Law enforcement officials made hurried efforts to assure locals that they were close to apprehending the alleged chicken thumper, beginning with a press briefing by the case officer, Deputy Tolan Retoll. As the deputy explained, detectives were already interviewing the neighbors of one Argosy Gothskillet, a local musician and habitual troublemaker with an 18 handicap. Said the deputy, "Neighbors remember him as a quiet, unassuming youngster, except for that weird Foghorn Leghorn tattoo."

(The perp's name isn't really Argosy Gothskillet. That would be silly. His real name is *Theodore* Gothskillet.)

Authorities admit, however, that they're still stumped as to Gothskillet's motive. Nobody's really buying any of the theories floating around the precinct -- that the kid was trying to get in the Guinness Book for "World's Biggest To-Go Bucket." And the chances of there being 1,000 simultaneous Cajun voodoo sacrifices in Fresno are pretty slim.

I have a different theory. I think the hens were whacked.

A thousand chickens, chip-shotted execution-style?

I think this was a hit job.

By the goat.

Barry Parham

I'm Sorry, Could You Think That Again?

Scientific breakthroughs vs. commercial breaks

<><><>~~~~~~~~~~~~~~~~~~~~~~~~~~<><><>

This last week, three historic events competed for the attention of humanity:

- Snookie had a baby
- Chelsea Clinton had a baby
- Neuroscientists demonstrated evidence of mind reading

I know -- it's hard for *me* to believe it, too, but it's true: somebody let the Clintons breed.

So, let's move on to less depressing events, like mind reading, or new gluten-free diets. According to an Australian "science news" website, the world's first-ever brain-to-brain message has been successfully transmitted during a series of carefully calibrated experiments performed by international researchers from France, Spain, and Harvard (a small country near Boston).

Barry Parham

The jubilant team of neuroscientists (*see related article: How to Detect Jubilation in People Who Wear Pocket Protectors*) are claiming they figured out a way to mentally send a single word from one person to another by making both people wear funny hats, a trick most of us mastered back in college, using tin foil and scientific amounts of beer.

The goal was to "communicate directly between two people by reading out the brain activity from one person and injecting brain activity into the second person," said one member of the team, a scientist whose title, no kidding, is all of this:

Alvaro (Al) Pascual-Leone, MD, PhD, Director of the Berenson-Allen Center for Noninvasive Brain Stimulation at Beth Israel Deaconess Medical Center (BIDMC) and Professor of Neurology at Harvard Medical School

To achieve their aim, here's what Al and his team did: they grabbed a guy in India, and after carefully lying to him, they talked the guy into wearing some kind of Mad Scientist hat with a mat of wires spiking out of it, making the guy look like Nick Nolte before coffee, except hungrier. According to the experiment Al had sketched out, Al intended to call this participant the "emitter," but none of the glee-filled neuroscientists could say "emitter" with a straight face.

The hat was a device known as a BCI, which stands for *Brain-to-Computer Interface*, unless you're Snookie, in which case it stands for *Babysit the child, idiot.* The subject straps the BCI onto his head, after which the device will allegedly interpret electrical

190

currents in the subject's brain. (In college, this is what we used to call a *taser*.)

By the way, Al refers to this interaction as a form of "Noninvasive Brain Stimulation," as opposed to, say, directly applying an electrical current to someone's face late one night at a frat house. (In college, this is what we used to call an *actionable offense*, usually followed by *jail time*.)

What happens next is that the guy with the hat thinks of a word, which generates electricity inside his skull, unless he's a politician. The BCI then grabs the electricity and translates it into some kind of binary code that Al calls Bacon's cipher, causing the other neuroscientists to choke back a giggle. (*see related article: Correlation Between Really Smart Guys and Heavy Drinking*)

Once the word's been encoded, Al's team sends the data over the Internet to another guy with a hat. (this guy's just known as the "receiver", because the team blew their whole Cool Terms budget on "emitter")

The receiver's hat, known as a *Computer-to-Brain Interface* or CBI (*see previous "budget" comment*), grabs the information from the internet and converts it to porn. Al's team then sells the porn to various federal agencies so their employees will have something to do at work in-between government shutdowns.

If I tried to tell you what happens next in the experiment, you wouldn't believe me, so ... well, I'll just quote the Australian article:

This device emits electrical pulses through the receiver's head, which make him 'see' flashes of light called phosphenes that don't actually exist.

Mmm hmm.

So let's review: we've got two guys electrocuting each other online, wearing weird hats, swapping images and seeing things that aren't there.

No wonder the story didn't make the headlines. This isn't breaking news ... this is just a normal Malibu weekend.

Hmm. Wonder if Brad Pitt's pregnant?

Bipeds Vs. Nopeds

I hate animals that don't need socks

Everybody has a favorite fear. Mine is snakes. Well, that, and the paralyzing thought of ever seeing Nancy Pelosi naked. Or clothed.

Snakes. I admit it. And I don't mean just a "don't watch this part of the movie" fear. I mean the kind of fear that makes you leap, reverse direction, accelerate in mid-air, and run into trees. The kind of fear that makes you shriek like Bill Clinton being told the rabbit died.

So. Now that I've fessed up, maybe you'll appreciate how irritated I am with the Universe at the moment -- not just for allowing a giant five-foot-long black snake to crawl through my front yard, but for then letting the foul disgusting slithering hell-spawn *climb a tree*.

A snake. Climbed a tree. In my yard.

Great. Now I gotta sell my house.

But Loki wasn't through with me. Two days later, I had this conversation with a landscaper.

~-~-~-~-~-~-~-~-~-~-~-~

Landscaper Guy: We've got gravel left over. Want me to spread some under the house?

Me: Sure. I'll get the key. Okay, there you go.

LG: Hey, is that a snake?

Me: [*muffled noise from half-way up a tree*]

LG: Yep, it's a cute little copperhead, stuck to that rodent glue trap.

Me: [*in a tree, on the phone to the realtor, in-between snorts of nitrous oxide*]

LG: Look! It's still alive!

Editor's Note: [*we apologize for the language we just heard from that tree*]

LG: Want me to put it in your trashcan?

Me: You do and I'll kill everybody in your family.
~-~-~-~-~-~-~-~-~-~-~-~

Remember the George Orwell novel, *1984*, and the terror that was Room 101? Once you were behind that door, Orwell's dystopian government would subject you to...well...

"You asked me once," said O'Brien, "what was in Room 101. I told you that you knew the answer already. Everyone knows it. The thing that is in Room 101 is the worst thing in the world."

...as Winston, Orwell's doomed protagonist, soon discovered when, in one of the most horrifying scenes in English literature, Winston was force-fed hour after excruciating hour of ... Hugh Grant movies.

Of course, it was hard to get too worked up over Winston; after all, the guy was named after a cigarette.

In my Room 101 there are reptiles.

Snakes. The worst thing in the world. In fact, if an interrogator ever made me watch movies starring snakes *and* Hugh Grant, I'd sing like Katherine the Great at the Kentucky Derby.

To be fair, I'm no fun for them, either. Even if a snake ever *did* manage to catch up with me after my initial twenty-mile sprint, the viper's venom wouldn't stand a chance -- I'd be dead from *fright*...not before *I* hit the floor, but before the *snake* did.

Dead on the ground...and *still*, my body would be trying to get away. Bystanders would respectfully point, noting, "Man. Look at that corpse *move!*"

But I've learned to accept it. My snake issues are a phobia way beyond the shackles of shame. It's not something I "manage." It'd be like me saying I was going to choose to stop digesting, or start producing plaid insulin, or suddenly develop a fondness for free-range tofu pizza.

I've learned to accept it, and to accept people's perceptions about it. Whenever my snake issues come up in conversation (or when a snake and I suddenly find ourselves in the same zip code), people usually respond in one of two ways:

~-~-~-~-~-~-~-~-~-~-~

Useless Advice

"Dude, if it weren't for snakes, you'd be overrun with mice and vermin."
Right. As if snakes weren't vermin.

"Hey, the snakes are more scared of *you*."
That is not mathematically possible. And stop talking to me like I was a grown-up.

"Just chop its head off!"
I can't chop heads off snakes. I've never found a store that has a knife with a hundred-yard handle.

See, when you're trying to give rational advice to someone with Snake Issues, you're about as welcome as one of those sun-cooked, crevice-jowled, Birkenstock-wearing, deodorant-shunning, pastel-smeared "artiste" pests who walk around in Arizona's 135-degree temps, wearing tongue jewelry and loose-fitting clothing, endlessly intoning "Yeah, but it's a *dry* heat."

~-~-~-~-~-~-~-~-~-~-~

Misplaced Camaraderie

'The only good snake is a dead snake."
Wrong, ace. I've seen those films of snakes reflexively trying to bite stuff ... *after its head was cut off.* Look, anything that can bite you *after* it's dead...

Another example: Let's say you're deathly afraid of, I don't know, clowns. So you pat my hand, nod knowingly, and say, "I know *just* how you feel! Me, I'm scared to death of clowns!"

Save it, Nurse Simpatico. I bet you've never had to watch a clown slither across your yard and climb a tree, have you? I thought not. Ever seen a clown under your house, stuck on a rodent glue trap? Hmm? *Hmm?*

~-~-~-~-~-~-~-~-~-~-~

I've learned to accept it. Occasionally, of course, someone will respond to my fang fear and loathing with simple scorn. Snarky derision. But it's usually a short-lived reaction, which generally ends right about the time they realize I've backed them into the glue trap.

197

Barry Parham

Reasonable People
(Sexual Harassment, Part I)
If the government managed sex, we'd all be sterile.
<><><>~~~~~~~~~~~~~~~~~~~~~~~~<><><>

Not long ago, I got to take an "workplace education" class called Sexual Harassment Awareness. I won't bore you with the back story about *why* I was in the class, but I'm pretty sure it had nothing to do with elevator cameras and my career in the NFL.

To be sure, whenever potential perps are being rounded up for sexual harassment complaints, I am a prime candidate.

Right.

I'm a single, five-decades-old, music-loving cynic with a mild addiction to tacos and Chinese takeaway. The last time I participated in anything remotely resembling sexual antics was after Hurricane Ivan hit Pensacola, when I helped a woman move a bed.

The sexual harassment class was nothing scary; just part of the annual activity spasm US corporations go through in an attempt to justify middle-management salaries...and to please their federal Uncle. Large US companies do these things because the large US government makes them do these things ... by threatening large non-compliance penalties ranging from stiff fines all the way up to making all the executives watch Al Gore documentaries.

And so, those that depend on these corporations for their weekly envelope also submit to awareness classes and other such yawners, for various altruistic reasons:

- they like to be seen as team players
- they wish to avoid offending anyone's sensibilities
- they have a mortgage

I did a little online research into the US government's role in Sexual Harassment law, just to find the funny parts, and because, for your average sex-crazed single satyr, I have an inordinate amount of spare time (to be fair, it's been a while since my last hurricane). And as usual, when dealing with D.C. I didn't have to look far to find stupid. Here are some actual quotes from government publications addressing Sexual Harassment Awareness:

~-~-~-~-~-~-~-~-~-~-~

Sexual harassment is specifically harassment of a sexual nature.

Didn't know that, did you, America? *Did you?*

Unwelcome behavior is just that; it is behavior that is not welcome.

I hear Congress is close to confirming what it is in salt water that makes it salty. (And if I know America, it won't be long before some victims group demands equal time for pepper water.)

Physical contact can include touching a woman's body.

On the other hand, touching the body of most guys I know quickly morphs into a business transaction, because money is usually offered. Not by the touch-*er* ... by the touch-*ee*.

Nobody is likely to harass someone they respect, either accidentally or deliberately.

How you accidentally respect someone, I have no idea.

Checking out people by looking them up and down can be uncomfortable to most people.

In fact, if they're really short, it can be downright difficult. Fortunately, it won't take long.

Other types of federally prohibited discrimination include harassment based on race, color, religion, gender, age, national origin, disability, and genetic information.

Genetic information? How do you even *do* that? Point to somebody's genome and giggle? Anybody got any good ribonucleic jokes?

~-~-~-~-~-~-~-~-~-~-~

One government website lists *Indicators that an Employee is Being Sexually Harassed.* According to the list, it might be a red flag if a co-worker "no longer joins in employee group activities." Hmm. I seem to remember a time when an employee of color named Rudolph no longer joined in any reindeer games, and I think Congress should look into this ... as soon as they get back from their five-week-long Labor Day weekend.

Another indicator that an employee is being sexually harassed is if they "suddenly start wearing very concealing/conservative clothes." By that definition, I suppose that anyone who shows up in a Tea Party turtleneck and a Reagan hoodie is simply screaming for intervention.

In the 90s, federal courts tried to modify the definition of Sexual Harassment to take into account any activity that "reasonable people" would find offensive. The "reasonable people" standard was first tested in the landmark civil rights case *Alice the Dominating Masseuse v. A Whole Bunch of Sailors*, but the designated Reasonable Person was deemed unreasonable when he demanded the Washington Redskins change their team name.

So it's a big deal, all this sexual harassment stuff. And don't make the mistake of thinking it's a one-way street, a street filled with female victims only, a street awash in women simultaneously driving and texting and talking and eating and sipping and making little pouty guppy faces while they touch up their makeup. In fact, of the 11,717 federal-level sexual harassment complaints received in 2010 by the EEOC, 16.4% were filed by guys. (Granted, over half of them were filed by the *same* guy, a troubled San Francisco street mime named Trixie who sells metrosexual Tupperware and runs a shelter for out-of-work stunt hamsters. But let's not niggle.)

In case you're wondering, I aced the Sexual Harassment course. Here's how: before taking the test, I got myself into a "victim mindset." I created a character in my head and tackled the test *as that character.* Suddenly, all the "could this scenario be considered sexual harassment?" questions became obvious, once I looked at each situation with the eyes of "Amber," an illegal immigrant single mom of color from Bolivia who's transgendered, disabled, depends on food stamps, and has a special-needs hamster.

Hey, don't knock it. It's my system, and it works. I aced the test, I bought some weed with the food stamps, and the hamster's finally mastering long division.

Plus, come April 15, Amber's tax deductions are gonna be *sweet.*

Barry Parham

How To Be True or False (Sexual Harassment, Part II)

Cynical Single Guy: 07, Political Correctness: 00

<><><>~~~~~~~~~~~~~~~~~~~~~~~~<><><>

Last week, I shared with you that I'd just completed a Sexual Harassment awareness course, a class I'd felt compelled to take for several reasons:

- The company that pays me a salary insisted.
- That salary keeps me from being homeless.
- Sleeping under a bridge is very overrated.

I also mentioned that the course was a normal annual thing that companies do, like giving salary reviews, or buying insanely expensive printers that hemorrhage ink and treat printer paper worse than Michael Vick trying to gladiator-train a pacifist poodle. And my name on the signup sheet was just one of many; it had nothing to with anything involving court orders, conditions of parole, or my messy pending divorce from both Angelina Jolie *and* Billy Bob Thornton. (don't laugh - at the rate they burn through spouses, it's just a matter of time before one of 'em gets to me)

Finally last week, I pointed out that I'd aced the Sexual Harassment course by reading each test question from the point-of-view of a Bolivian woman named Amber. (don't tell Angelina)

And now, just in case you'd like a little monitor of your own Sexual Harassment sensitivity, we've mocked up a quick quiz: some sample scenarios, each describing a situation that may or may not be considered "actionable" sexual harassment, which is a very serious legal claim that could lead to disastrous results, like losing your job, or Andrew Weiner texting you a lewd selfie.

Ready? Let's begin.

~-~-~-~-~-~-~-~-~-~-~

Ed set an email to a workmate, complimenting the co-worker on having purchased an attractive new dress.

Question: Given that Ed is a defensive back in the NFL, who bought a dress?

~-~-~-~-~-~-~-~-~-~-~

Joanne, a financial analyst, has to work with Terrance, the idiot in charge of buying printers, at least when he's not standing in the office hallways swinging an imaginary golf club. Terrance likes to talk about himself during his wildly popular ink cartridge demos, and Joanne's not the only employee who finds his stories offensive.

Joanne takes Terrance aside and asks him to stop. Not only does Terrance not stop his boasting after Joanne's request, but he starts peppering his PowerPoint demos with photos from National Geographic.

Question: Just how flexible is the "justifiable" part of "justifiable homicide?"

~-~-~-~-~-~

At the office where Roberto works, the men gather around the water cooler at break time, swapping lies and laughing loudly. One day, a woman walks in. The guys' laughter subsides, they stare at her, and Roberto says, "Sally, you look lovely today."

Question: What is Sally doing in the break room naked?

~-~-~-~-~-~-~-~-~

John and Lois from Sales travel together on a week-long business trip. During the taxi ride from the airport, John snuggles up to Lois and tries to hold her hand. Lois strongly objects, but John won't back off.

By the time the taxi reaches the hotel, John is unconscious and Lois has extracted several of his teeth with a company-branded staple remover.

Question: Should Lois tip the driver?

~-~-~-~-~-~

Roberta, an Account Rep, tells her assistant, Alex, that the only way he can keep his job is by having sex with her. This type of sexual harassment is what's called *quid pro quo*, which translates roughly as "show me your quid and I'll make you a pro."

Question: I used to work in sales. How come this stuff never happens to *me?*

~-~-~-~-~-~

William, the sales manager, gets drunk and exposes himself to several women at the company picnic. The next day William apologizes, but his bawdy behavior becomes a habit.

Question: Should William run for the House or the Senate?

~-~-~-~-~-~

While at work, Janet frequently makes personal phone calls to her friends. Her conversations are loud and generously sprinkled with sexually explicit language. Her co-workers in nearby cubicles cannot help but overhear her conversations.

Question: Anybody got Janet's phone number?

~-~-~-~-~-~

Day after day, Mary publicly badgers Tony to sign her "Boycott Chick-fil-A" petition. Tony disagrees with Mary that the fast food chain's owner should have to apologize for personal religious beliefs. Mary insists that Chick-fil-A is a hate-filled cauldron of narrow-minded bigots, while she orders a gluten-free tofu enchilada at her whites-only tennis club.

Question: How'd you like to be the poor schmuck that married Mary?

~-~-~-~-~-~

Steve and Ray have worked together for many years at the Georgia State Prison for Recidivist Women Midgets. Recently, during the mid-day Buddy Checks, Ray has started to make suggestive comments to Steve about his physique, including giving parts of Steve's physique cute nicknames, like Hannibal, Canine Lucy, and Peter Tush. Ray has also hinted that he would like to go away with Steve for a weekend sometime, maybe to a Gay Pride schnapps-a-thon at an Aspen Tranq Bar. Steve has told Ray that he's not interested in him that way and has asked Ray to stop, except for the schnapps. Ray eventually transfers to a different department, where he develops an intimate relationship with a taupe-stained paint roller tube.

Question: Why won't those haters at Chick-fil-A sell gay schnapps?

~-~-~-~-~-~

Joan and Steve enjoy a great working relationship and just recently have started dating. They can't seem to get enough of each other outside of the workplace. At work, however, they usually only interact during breaks and lunch, which they take together. They are clearly infatuated with each other but do not engage in public displays of affection.

Question: Has anybody told Ray?

~-~-~-~-~-~-~-~-~-~-~-~

Honey, Where's My Mantra?

It's our annual Divine Empowerments 2-For-1 sale!

<><><>~~~~~~~~~~~~~~~~~~~~~~~<><><>

Not long ago, I told you about Dr. Skippy. And, having said that, I realize something sobering -- I've lived a long full life, but I may have outlived my cultural usefulness if all I have left to offer literature is sentences like "Not long ago, I told you about Dr. Skippy."

What can I say? Sometimes, when you open life's oyster, there's no pearl of wisdom in there. Just some grit.

That's my gift to you. A grit of wisdom.

As you'll recall, Dr. Skippy also peddles in wisdom grits, of a sort. Dr. Skippy is one of those consciousness gurus that infest the internet ... and the deep discount bins at Barnes & Noble ... one of those self-anointed saviors claiming to hold the keys that will unlock awareness, enhance self-actualization, and unscramble HBO.

What drew me to check out Dr. Skippy was this comment from his website: "For more than four hundred million years, I have protected the borders between the physical world and the worlds of shadow." So here's a guy who's somewhere north of 400 million years old, and still calling himself "Skippy." Most guys will drop the cheesy yearbook nicknames once they reach age two hundred million or so. I mean, if you're older than the oceans, or Strom Thurmond, it's time to let go of salad days monikers like *Skippy*, *Tater*, *Hollow Leg*, or *Voted Most Likely To Be Recidivist*.

I'm kidding, of course. Dr. Skippy isn't his *real* name. (His real name is *Ed* Skippy.) "Dr. Skippy" is just a pseudonym I made up to protect the innocent. No, not innocent *him*; innocent *me*. Look, if it turns out that Ed's as good as he says he is, he might have lawyers on retainer in several different dimensions. Being sued is bad enough; but being sued in an alternate universe where you haven't even been born yet? Ain't nobody got space-time for that.

In any event, Dr. Skippy offers several solutions in your search for cosmic oneness, each pathway accessible through a series of holistic interactions with your credit card (trans-universal service charges may apply). At Der Skipster's website, you can browse a broad assortment of books, CDs, attunements, amulets (literally, "little amuls"), verbenas (small verbs), and healing stones (Mick Jagger action figure sold separately). And all at discount prices! (divine empowerments not included)

Still not self-activated sated? Rubbing a British rock musician on your verbena not your cup of chai tea? No worries - Dr. Skippy to the rescue! The doctor highly recommends you round out your self-awareness regime with frequent visits to the groaningly-named, guru-rich getaway -- The

ConsciousNest. (winner of the 2009 Beads, Birkenstocks & Body Odor Award for Worst Self-Help Pun)

A nurturing community and fully-cloaked Section 501(c)(3) tax shelter, The ConsciousNest - or *The Nest*, as it's known to fans and the Non-Profit Wing watchdogs at the IRS - is the go-to source for time-tested New Age modalities, like Reiki Reflexology (basically, some patchouli-scented chick pokes your feet with her thumbs), Chakra Balancing With Tuning Forks (great for Grandma's stressed-out spinet!), and Quantum Touch. (we'll not get into the details here, but it's illegal in five Southern States)

Among their other positively-vibrating positives:

- They come highly recommended by a 400-million-year-old border guard
- They almost never run out of amulets
- They're located in Cleveland, because when I think *holistic spiritual healing*, I think Cleveland

It's a safe bet to claim that The ConsciousNest is a high point in the heady glitz and glamour that is Cleveland, that dazzling jewel of the Rust Belt. Any time the topic is to-die-for tourist destinations, The Nest is part of what keeps Cleveland consistently ranking somewhere between Burma and Snuff Bucket, Arkansas. But don't take *my* word for it. Let's meet the staff!

Mallow is a Shamanic Practitioner who specializes in "burying all the dead baggage that weighs you down." And from the looks of her, when Mallow says *bury*, Mallow means *eat*.

213

Lola can remove your body's negative energy and replace it with positive energy color, using energy from Mother Earth and tax-deductible tins of Rit dye. Lola refers to herself a "wonderful channel," but other members of The Nest staff call her a "tool."

Kamehameha Kahiapo Jones performs table and chair massage at The Nest. This could explain why all their furniture has that weird peaceful expression.

Once a month, The Nest is honored to host **Jose Khanyusea** (formerly of Jolistic Jealing with Jose), who heals using intuitive readings and, in drastic cases, tuning forks. In his bio, Jose recommends you "book" a session during his "office hours." We don't "know" why Jose wraps "quotation marks" around pedestrian terms like "book" and "office hours." Perhaps Jose is an "undocumented shaman" or, to use the politically correct term, an "illegal sun alien." We suggest you "call" Jose before he gets "caught," because once that jappens, Jose could be "doing time."

Uvula Corona is the most popular Reflexologist at The Nest (the place is practically *dripping* with Reflexologists). One testimonial began: "I call hers 'the butter touch.' I am normally very ticklish, but with Uvula..." That's how the testimonial *began*, anyway. We don't know how it ended, cause at that point we had to stop reading it. We were beginning to feel unclean.

~-~-~-~-~-~-~-~-~-~-~

Winding Down Civilization

Well, we hope you've found this week's self-help help helpful. So get your Gaia on; grab a knife and tuning fork and feed your inner child; align your crystals and feng your shui; resonate your Reiki; stare at the sun.

Just be careful with that Quantum Touch.

You could go blind.

Barry Parham

Astro-Physical Graffiti

Life is but a screen.

<><><>~~~~~~~~~~~~~~~~~~~~~~~~~<><><>

Okay, what's wrong with the following sentence?

"Operating out of a trailer in rural Illinois, government researchers are experimenting to determine if our reality is really just a great big hologram."

You're right. That wasn't a fair question. Practically *everything* is wrong with that sentence.

- It can't be in a trailer. In many Midwestern states, state law requires that all mobile homes maintain an active meth lab.
- "Government research" is mismanaged by everybody, accountable to nobody, and expensive for the wrong people. Plus, it tends to result in monumental missteps, like federally-restricted toilet flushes, or the UN.
- Given the tepid state of our economy, I don't see how we can afford to fund psychotic "Do We Live In The Matrix?" research *and* simultaneously support

federally-funded grants that pay scientists to coax shrimp onto treadmills and measure their stress. (the shrimps' stress, not the scientists')

- If a federal agency is running some op out of a rural Illinois trailer, another federal agency could confuse it with a meth lab, and then the government might arrest itself.

- Not that *that's* a bad thing.

- The whole hologram premise is silly, haphazard, and functionally useless, much like Obama's foreign policy.

- On the other hand, if our government's using our tax money to see if we're all just reflections in some alien's hologram, I guess the "that's just silly" ship sailed long ago.

But apparently it's happening. According to an online article at vice.com (yes, there is), government employees are busily trying to prove that you're not real, except on April 15. You, and everyone you know, might be nothing more than overworked, overweight characters in some cosmic kid's video game. The universe is just one huge PlayStation, with a really long extension cord.

This includes everything you think is real: the feel of your child's cheek; the color blue; the smell of bacon; Hollywood indignation; official statements from the White House.

The group in charge of this research gets their beer money from the Department of Energy's Fermilab Center for Particle Astrophysics, which is in the same building as the DoE's Algae-Powered Automobile Research Lab (yes, there is) and just down the hall from the Bureau of Fracking And Other

Words That Sound Dirty But Aren't (probably not, but I wouldn't be a bit surprised).

According to the gang at Fermilab, reality is like a game, with a game screen, and the screen only has a limited amount of intelligence at any one time, as if reality were John Kerry in mid-sentence. Team Fermi claims that if you were able to zoom in close enough, you'd be able to glimpse the "pixels" of the universe. (this also works if you zoom in close enough to John Kerry)

That's your tax dollars at work. Federal monies lavished on adult boys who spent their childhoods clutching game controllers in dark basements. These are the fashion-awkward dweebs you knew in college who were always trying to sneak up on the light inside the refrigerator.

The trailer-bound team is hoping to resolve long-standing incongruities between Albert Einstein's theory of relativity (*never lend money to your relatives*) and Max Planck's packet-based model of quanta (*an Australian airline*). Unfortunately, the federally-funded goobers are coming at giants like Einstein and Planck with existential ammo of this caliber: "The natural world behaves exactly the same way as the environment of *Grand Theft Auto IV*."

Well, that *is* breaking news. The cosmos is just a crime scene; the Big Bang was based on downtown Detroit.

And the Red Bull & Doritos-diet crowd are claiming some rather bold discoveries.

"It's not every day you wake up and learn something that happened a trillionth of a trillionth of a trillionth of a second after the beginning of the universe," said Mort Kanioskowalski, an astrophysicist who sadly was not involved with the hologram team because they couldn't fit his whole name on the grant. However, as acknowledgement for his "megaskillionth of a second" observation, Mort was awarded the 2014 Nobel Prize for Understatement.

Personally, I just want to see the guy's watch.

The Fermicelli are structuring their experiments around an array of old plastic surgery lasers bought at auction from Michael Jackson's estate, and padding their documentation with pickup lines and quantum buzzwords used at astrophysicist singles bars.

~-~-~-~-~-~-~-~-~-~-~

"Hi, cutie. What's your valence?"

"Schrödinger's cat walks into a bar. Or not."

"Stop me if you'll eventually have heard this one..."

"So. You localize your wave function here with a statistically significant regularity?"

"Schrödinger's cat walks into a bar. The bartender asks, 'Can I see some ID?' The cat replies, 'Okay, but it may have expired.'"

"Girl, you need to stop! Don't you know curvature like yours could sublimate gravity?"

"What say we get outta here and go somewhere quiet where I can talk."

"Schrödinger walks into a bar. The bartender says, 'What'll it be?' Schrödinger replies, 'Hard to say.'"

"Why am I staring? Look, in quantum mechanics, particles don't have a definite state unless they're being observed. So *I'm* doing *you* a favor."

~-~-~-~-~-~-~-~-~-~-~

And then it hit me. The scenario these holistic hologramaniacs are trying to prove is this:

What if you could step outside yourself, rise up into the sky, and see yourself in a simulation where you were stepping outside yourself, rising up into the sky, and seeing yourself in a simulation? Which you is real?

Well, I have a news flash for the kids at Quantum Trailer Park. Mankind already has one of those. It's called Google Earth.

You're welcome.

Now hand over the Doritos.

Barry Parham

The Mental Home Shopping Network

My, what acute angina!

I saw a fluff piece on the news the other day that provides yet another answer to one of humankind's burning questions: Why aren't we ever visited by intelligent life forms from other planets?

There's a reason.

Aliens read the reviews.

See, aliens do their homework. (They're not called "intelligent life forms" for nothing, you know.) Before setting off on a space-folding family holiday, with all the clones (kids) and the family dog (Lunar Rover), extra-terrestrials take the time to scope things out. Prior to checking the tires and topping off the anti-matter tank, galactic travellers research the destination ... and the route, too, given the distances between deep space freeway exits.

Barry Parham

Before committing, cosmic Moms will at least megaGoogle the candidate planet, even if the planet boasts an "Alien World" theme park in some faraway place called Or-Land Of Lorida. After all, if the theme park's host planet is unstable, there's no need to exchange currency, stow a few dozen fission energy breakfast bars, and stock up on SPF 4,000,000,000 sun screen.

ET phone references.

And no self-respecting alien with one or more heads is gonna bother visiting a world described in the travel brochure as "awfully petty."

The news piece I saw wasn't about anything. It was just fluff ... typical slow-news-day drivel ... just something to fill the dead air in-between updates on which bogus indignation groups are more offended by the names of football teams.

Just another yawner about stupid people looking to excuse being stupid by suing other people for making them be stupid.

Here's the story:

As it turns out, there's a new reality show called *Dating Naked*, proving conclusively that TV executives, as a sentient life form, have officially had their last idea. The show revolves around several couples who have no clothes and even less luck at dating -- they're more desperate than an Apple store in Amish country.

As the more clever readers will have inferred from the show's catchy title, the cast is naked. The network (VH1) collected these contestants, riffed through all the consent forms from legal, and dumped the kids on a beach someplace, where they all walk around comparing, um, résumés, until everybody settles on a mate and pairs off.

So, of course, one of the naked contestants is now suing the show because they filmed her ... ready? ... naked.

That detail *alone* probably cost Earth untold trillions in space alien tourist income.

Now, in the interest of full disclosure, let me say that I haven't seen the show, because I have no interest in full disclosure. Before I'd murder a perfectly innocent evening by watching naked morons, Id rather read the contents label from a can of motor oil. But this lawsuit story did yield some valuable insights:

- VH1, the music video channel, hasn't actually shown a music video since 1989
- Motor oil may be the only product in America that doesn't contain peanut products
- Five seconds ago, I wrote about murdering an evening, and I've already been contacted by six lawyers

I did, however, get to see some still shots from the show while researching this story online. In one scene, a clad-less couple were playing naked croquet, completely devoid of propriety, not to mention pockets. Both the dude and the dudette wore socks and shoes, which technically qualifies as naked, according to Hoyle's International Rules & Regulations For Lawn Games Involving Naked People Swinging Mallets. In addition, the female sported a tasteful, broad-brimmed white hat, as if she were attending the Kentucky Derby at Jack Nicholson's house.

~-~-~-~-~-~-~-~-~-~-~

Actually, it was a bit refreshing to see such a standard, old-school throwback -- a couple comprised of exactly one male and one female ... one doe and one buck, buck-naked or no.

Gender in America, it seems, has become something you can just buy, like a hat, or a politician. And as with any purchase, there are options. At a famous San Francisco eatery, I'm told there are separate bathrooms for thirteen distinct genders, including fairly severe choices, like "Not Applicable" and "Nancy Pelosi." These days, we've got so many gender options in America that the old stand-by plotline "boy meets girl" is just as likely to be "boy becomes girl, girl fathers child with self, child runs off with sparkly vampire."

~-~-~-~-~-~-~-~-~-~-~

Now. Here's the lawsuit part. Yes, the show is called *Dating Naked*, and yes, the contestants had packed really, really lightly, other than some socks and the occasional Audrey Hepburn hat. But even in today's ultra-permissive culture, where two transgendered women can marry a yak, there are still things you can't show on television. We call these things "*erogenous zones*," from the Latin word for "*That stunt's gonna cost you your broadcast license.*"

226

Winding Down Civilization

The way the show's producers planned to get around the TV taboos was by digitally blurring the more poetic areas of the contestants' unevenly tanned bodies.

(Imagine *that* plum job - blurring people's private parts. Don't you know *there's* a guy who never gets to year's end with an unused sick day.)

But in one scene, according to the naked-dating-game plaintiff, Joe the Blur Guy missed a spot. As one British writer put it, "the producers failed to blur her modesty."

In other words, little Victoria suddenly had no more Secrets.

And so now, the biologically-correct victim is suing the show for $10 million, possibly so she can buy a bigger hat. (Joe the Blur Guy will be fine. He's a card-carrying member of the Modesty Blurring union, Local #414.)

Of course, the in-focus incident immediately went viral, and as you can imagine, the internet staged an all-you-can-tweet insult buffet. I personally can think of about 1,800 jokes, which I'll share with you some day, if I'm ever reincarnated and come back as a guy without parents that I have to face on Thanksgiving.

And here's the best part of all: in addition to her other actionable losses, the chick says the no-blur slip-up cost her a relationship, because ever since her little south quadrant selfie appeared online, the guy she'd been dating has stopped returning her calls.

Seriously. The squirrely twit is on a TV show, naked, picking out a naked guy to date, and she can't figure out why her boyfriend back home won't pick up the phone.

It's gonna be a long cold winter down at Alien World.

The Chicken Soup Nazi

Global thermonuclear war. It just ain't what it used to be.

<><><>~~~~~~~~~~~~~~~~~~~~~~~~<><><>

The breaking point in the Ukrainian sanctions, apparently -- the solomy that broke the camel's pozvonochnik -- was when America cut off Russia's access to Disney World. After all, for decades the Soviet Old Boy network had been getting the wink from US border officials as junketing Russians presented their counterfeit "Florida Resident" all-access passes.

Plus, they'd finally learned how to pronounce *splash-tacular.*

But then, as the US President was busily performing his sacred Presidential duties on a recent weekday, he shanked a fairway shot, got all pouty, and decided to punish somebody. And this time, he picked Vladimir Putin. (this is known as "leading from behind")

Putin, of course, responded forcefully; after all, he is famous for raw diplomatic flourish, often being photographed riding a horse without a shirt (Putin, not the horse). So when the US Golfer-in-Chief got snippy, Big Vlad countered with a list of grocery items that Russia would no longer purchase from America.

(Fortunately, however, there's hope for the good guys. Right now, Jack Bauer is somewhere in Russia, chained inside a box, trying to escape in time for the Fall season.)

And there, in a nutshell, is the current version of what was once larger-than-life geopolitical leadership: the leader of America whips out a red crayon, and the leader of Russia parries with a no-shopping list.

Earth's mightiest combatants -- a grinning golf fanatic and a half-naked ex-spook.

And all the free world's hopes lie with an imaginary character played by the son of Hawkeye Pierce from M*A*S*H.

So there we were. The Epcot Gambit. And that's when the Cold War got hot, as Putin uttered those light-dimming, soul-numbing, apocalyptic words:

"No more chicken for you!"

And there they were: the two one-time titans of the Twentieth Century, facing off in...a food fight. Suddenly, the SALT talks were actually about salt. SDI, replaced by HDL.

~-~-~-~-~-~-~-~-~-~-~

Meanwhile, in Iraq...
After three-putting the eighth green, the US President got steamed and authorized humanitarian air drops over Iraq. Vice

President Joe Biden heartily approved the action, stating for the record that everybody should have air. Then he cursed for a few minutes before his keepers got the restraints back on.

~-~-~-~-~-~-~-~-~-~

Poultry will lead the banned foods list, according to Transnational Dynamics experts at the National Chicken Council, a group that regularly studies geopolitical interplay, and barbecue sauce. And the American economy *will* take a hit. After all, as every non-ADHD-medicated schoolchild knows, Russia is the second largest importer of US chicken. (This does not factor in sales of sacrificial chickens to Haitian churches. Or Chicago baseball teams. Which is the same thing.)

Interestingly, the second most-imported item on the Russian Bear's nyet-nyet list is pistachios. I know that'll be hard news to swallow for those nursing the US economy, particularly investors whose stock portfolios are pistachio-heavy, but it's *great* news for the peanut sector. According to a spokesperson for the American Peanut Council, the Russian ban "does not include peanuts, raw or processed." Of course, that statement leads to two sobering acknowledgements:

1) We may soon be facing a wildly speculative, Wall Street-threatening pistachio glut
2) We can't fund space exploration, but there's an American Peanut Council

But let's be realistic, America. As a food group, peanuts are practically an endangered species in America, because Americans simply can't eat them. Sometime in the last quarter-century, every wide-eyed kid in this country somehow

231

developed death-dealing peanut allergies. You can't buy *anything* anymore - not a breakfast bar, not a ham sandwich, not a gluten-free Russian bride - without checking the label for the dread alert:

FOOD ALLERGY WARNING: MAY CONTAIN PEANUT OR TREE NUT PRODUCTS

We are pitiful. We are wimpifed. And all of us over the age of forty know when the Great American Wimpification began. We know what happened.

It all started to go downhill when our obscenely bloated "Helicopter Mom" federal government started censoring all the over-the-top violence from Roadrunner and Tom & Jerry cartoons. All those mallets to the head; all that squashing; all those Acme safes falling from the sky -- all that ridiculous toon violence served a purpose. It was a vaccination, a holistic way of training our immune systems. Whacking Wile E. Coyote, week after week, made us strong. As a result, we now have a nation full of little wimpy kids who can longer lunch on peanut butter & jelly.

~-~-~-~-~-~-~-~-~-~-~

Meanwhile, in Washington, DC...
The IRS scandal keeps heating up. And now, some desk rat over at Health & Human Services is being looked at as a future felon, accused of destroying emails *from an entirely different department!* Apparently, IRS emails were vanishing so fast, they had to pull in other departments to assist in the shredding.
~-~-~-~-~-~-~-~-~-~-~

So, despite all the menu-limiting machinations from Putin's Evil Empire, peanuts are gonna be fine. And, to be honest, the fear of plummeting chicken sales causing another downward economic spiral in the States is likely overblown, too. Should stock of biddies begin to back up at the chicken ranch docks, some Senator from a McNugget-dependent State will start jumping up and down, screaming about the vital role bantams play in a vibrant national security policy, and the federal government will simply subsidize chicken.

And besides, if there *is* a chicken overpopulation crisis, Americans will rise to the occasion. For example, Chick-fil-A will undoubtedly do its part with pullet discounts for its valued customers, as long as they're not gay. (the chickens, not the customers)

~-~-~-~-~-~-~-~-~-~-~

Meanwhile, at the US border...

Vice President Joe Biden gnawed through his mask, found an open mike, and made this psychotic pronouncement: "These [60,000 illegal immigrants] are not somebody else's kids. These are our kids."

I can already see the real estate ad.

WANTED: Home in suburban Delaware with 30,000 bedrooms and a very, very serious laundry. Smallpox containment facility a plus.

Thanks for handling it, Joe! Good luck with all the adoptions.

And if you and the kids need any chicken, sing out.

Barry Parham

We Had It Tough

A bit of perspective for Generation X-Pects

<><><>~~~~~~~~~~~~~~~~~~~~~~~~~~~<><><>

Here's what the creature said:

"Dude, this is so lame. I barely got two bars!"

I was in the mall food court, because sometimes nothing else will do but a genetically confused pseudo-gyro, heated in a discount microwave oven set on "Tepid," then served in crumpled wax paper from an entirely different restaurant and eaten at a damp cabaret table hurriedly wiped down by a relapsed wino with a sepia-crusted rag that's already been squeegeed across 475 other tables since it was last rinsed out on the first of the month in a bucket stored on the floor of a poorly-lit closet shared with the Cambodian owners of a recently-indicted discount aquarium and lunch buffet.

Okay, the first of *last* month.

The creature was some once-or-future male from Generation Lax, raccoon-eyed with mascara, his face punched full of holes and with a mid-sized novel tattooed along one arm, complaining to his equally adorned co-Goth about the lousy Wi-Fi coverage.

The *free* Wi-Fi coverage.

Aw. Boo bloody hoo. Captain Hepatitis has a free, untethered connection that grants him instantaneous, unlimited access to the most colossal, free-of-charge information network in the history of mankind, but it still isn't fast enough to suit Freak of Nature Boy's perceived needs, which sadly didn't include bathing.

Speaking as a product of the 50s, it amazes me when I hear today's kids complaining. And when I say "kids," I don't just mean "minors." I mean anybody under the age of Woodstock; anybody too young to remember who hosted the first episode of *Saturday Night Live* (George Carlin); anybody too young to remember that, once upon a time, the only people doing a "moon walk" were highly-trained heroes from NASA.

And they wore *two* gloves.

Now, I'm not one of those people who pine for younger days. I don't want to do it all again, especially that part where, one day on the way home from high school, I changed my mind about turning right and made a hard left from the far right lane, to the great surprise of several cars behind me.

Well, they were behind me *originally*.

And I don't spend my senior solar cycles sighing wistfully, "Oh, if only I knew *then* what I know *now*." Don't be silly. If I was stuck back then, but knew what I know now, I'd be yelling at the TV every Monday night because *24* was supposed to be on.

We had it tough. But these kids today, they don't realize how good they've got it. Heck, compared to life in America today, we were practically Sparta. Without all the cool mystique. And all the hot chicks.

Yeah, we had it tough. Here: let's call up the recall. Let's have a look in the rearview.

Witness:

- Back when I was a chap, we had to write. No, not type...*write*. No, not text acronyms with two thumbs...write *whole words*, with our *whole hands*.
- And we had to use things nobody uses anymore: things like spelling; punctuation; grammar; leeches.
- To get money, we had to actually go *inside* the bank.
- We had to eat meals, as a family, at home. Until the advent of a radical new thing called White Castle, there was no such thing as "fast food." The closest we ever got to fast food was when some genius thought of putting peanut butter and jelly in the same jar.
- After White Castle, of course, came McDonald's, but those mass-produced personality vacuums McReplicated so fast they weren't so much a "chain" as they were a virus. (McDonald's slogan: *Over 60 billion served, and we're still on our first pound of ground beef*)
- People today still use the expression "roll down your window." But once upon a time, *you had to actually roll the window down*. Seriously. If you wanted to raise or

237

lower your window in the family car, you had to crank a geared handle. Of course, the down side was that when a parent at home would command, "raise the thermostat," the more stupid children would dash about the room, looking for a crank.

- Nobody, like, ever used the word "like" more than, like, once in, like, a whole sentence and stuff. In fact, if you did, literate people would look at each other, wink, and then suggest you raise the thermostat.

- We only had two genders. These days, it's practically a buffet. The last list I saw offered fourteen gender options, including "Not Applicable" and "Rosie O'Donnell."

- TV channels. There were four. *Maybe*. Nowadays, we have more TV channels than we have genders. *Barely*. And ultra-niche channels they are, too! For example, there's a whole cable channel dedicated to Single Suburban Atheist Cross-dressing Vampire Surrogate Parents Who Are Paleo-Gluten-Free And Raise Methodist-Leaning Jack Russell Terriers.

- And speaking of entertainment...what's happened to music? Back in the day, music wasn't so angry. Today we have bands with horrible, frightening names like Slayer, Megadeth, and John Tesh; we have bitter genres like Crust Punk, Anarcho Punk, and Rod Stewart Doing Covers of Frank Sinatra Doing Covers of The Beatles. Back in the day, the most violent we ever got was something called the British Invasion. (We did have The Kinks, but that didn't make people rush out to create fourteen genders.)

- True, in 1969 the Rolling Stones did come out with an album named *Let It Bleed*, but marketing called and made them tone it down, so the *Let It Bleed* album cover ended up just being a picture of a nice frosted cake.

- It goes without saying that there was no internet yet. On the bright side, there was no Al Gore yet, either.

- Or email. Of course, email's *already* old school. Today's no-attention-span spoilees have to have *instant* messaging, so that when a person posts on facebook that they're "driving to the store lol" people will get the news *immediately*. Critical life-changing personal updates like that now have to travel so fast that we've decided our antiquated vocabulary just slows things down. Whole words are way too long. So we've come up with an abbreviated language that uses words like r and u and ur and 2, until it seems like the whole planet is constantly reciting license plates.

See? Back then, we didn't even have email. So if you wanted to share a joke, you had to literally go find another person and tell them the joke.

But back then, we never knew if the joke was funny. These days, everybody knows how to *type* LOL, but when I was a kid, nobody knew how to *say* it.

We had it tough.

Barry Parham

Hobby Lobbying

Retail misogyny? There's an app for that!

<><><>~~~~~~~~~~~~~~~~~~~~~~~~~<><><>

It's official. The gavel has dropped, and dark days await the women of America. For lo, the Supreme Court hath spoken: from now on, women can no longer have sex at Hobby Lobby.

It's confirmed. The evil executives at retail giant Hobby Lobby hate women ... assuming we can believe all the shrill outrage recently from Prius-loads of over-excited "reproductive rights" advocates who've sworn off gluten, and deodorant.

Evidently, those heartless Hobby Lobby moneychangers have declared all-out war on women, a move which, based on the average composition of a Hobby Lobby check-out line, is a bold move indeed.

Have you ever *seen* a Hobby Lobby check-out line? Ninety-nine-point-something-something-percent women ... and formidable female specimens at that. I wouldn't want to use the pejorative term "large," so let's just say these are women with a very low center of gravity.

241

And these patrons are retail warriors; these are Women On A Mission. Steel-eyed lasses in comfortable shoes, shepherding a caravan of two or three bulging carts, sometimes more, practically throbbing with wreath supplies, monogrammed navel lint brushes, and complex pre-constructed home decorating risks that are bigger than my first apartment. Once, not long ago, I was waiting to check out with my meager scoff-inducing payload of two whole candles, and the lady in front of me had in her cart what appeared to be the entire hull of a mid-sized naval vessel -- but the thing was punched full of square openings, each with a little rail, and the entire substructure painted to look like climbing ivy. I finally decided it was either a very ambitious bird feeder, or else a "storm the admin building" simulator and the woman was planning to seize a Nicaraguan university using tiny little Contra gerbils.

I'm just glad I wasn't stuck behind her on Double Coupon Day.

But now that Hobby Lobby has gone rogue and started slaying women in the streets, I may have to find a new place to buy candles.

All right, calm down. *Of course* I'm kidding. Nobody's slaying anybody in the streets.
... ...
They take the women behind the store and *then* slay them. (they lure the women with promises of double coupons)

In fact, Hobby Lobby's brutal take-no-prisoners war on women targets *employees*, not customers. Nor is it true that women at Hobby Lobby are shopping during sex, though I'm sure some women could pull that off. Personally, I've never witnessed a live act of non-Protestant intimacy at a Hobby Lobby.

But I bet you'll think twice the next time you hear "Clean-up, aisle seven."

No, all this recent media uproar is about women who work for Hobby Lobby having to pay for their own birth control -- because, as every patriotic American knows, free birth control is an inalienable human right, enumerated in the US Constitution and listed just after free cellphones, taxpayer-subsidized hi-def cable TV, and the right to leave your car idling in the drop-off lane outside the airport.

See, it all started when America's Golf Pro-in-Chief alchemied a health care plan so gloriously comprehensive that even middle-aged women could now get circumcised. Finally, sixty-year-old soccer (grand)moms were gonna be eligible for maternity care, and there would be free birth control for nuns.

It was a ~~power grab~~ piece of legislation so ~~invasive~~ kindhearted that only one ~~thug posse~~ federal agency had the ~~jack-booted storm-troopers~~ tender caretaker skills necessary to ~~unleash the madness~~ administer its mercies: that paragon of compassion ... the IRS. And it was a law so wildly popular that the government had to make it illegal for anybody to *not* buy it.

Then, suddenly, those priggish Puritans at Ye Olde Hobbie Lobbie said, "Hey. Wait a minute. Look, the IRS wing of the AMA says we have to pay for our employees' birth control --

which includes sixteen different medications or treatments. But four of the sixteen medications are designed to be taken *after the woman is pregnant*, and we don't believe in abortion, except in the case of IRS auditors. So here's what we'll do: we'll pay for twelve of the sixteen birth control methods. Fair enough?"

Of course not. Enter Sandra Fluke.

In case you haven't heard of her, Sandra Fluke is an ex-law student whose claim to fame was being the first woman in America whose birth control spending exceeds the Gross National Product of Brazil. And perhaps for that very reason, femme la Fluke thinks her contraceptive costs should be paid for by somebody else. *(see US Constitution) (You won't find a "gimme free stuff" section in there, but that's never stopped these people)*

And so, when Hobby Lobby dared to stand between Sandra and her sisters-in-sexual-solidarity, Ms. Fluke took a break from her busy birth-control-intensive hobby to wail about how Hobby Lobby was using NRA assault weapons to kidnap uncircumcised grandmothers and then push them off cliffs where they fell into a conservative wood chipper donated by George Bush.

(Not that the Fluke was actually *working* at Hobby Lobby, or anywhere else, for that matter. When you have a hobby that requires that much contraception, you don't have *time* for a job.)

But sadly, despite all the rabid victim-wailing from little Sandra and her big Pile O' Hormones, we now learn that the Supreme Court has ruled in favor of the big, bad retailers. And so, it's over. By this time next week, thanks to Hobby Lobby, every woman in America will be dead.

But look on the bright side -- check-out lines will be way faster on Double Coupon Day.

Barry Parham

Poor is the new Rich

How to succeed at failing to succeed

<><><>~~~~~~~~~~~~~~~~~~~~~~~~~<><><>

Work.

When Earthlings finally come up with a "Most Overrated Thing Ever" award, work will win. In fact, I'm ready to not do it anymore, just as soon as I figure out how to kick a few persistent personal habits, like wearing clothes. And eating.

(I could just stop eating, of course, but that usually leads to being dead, after which you have to vote in North Carolina.)

Until then, I'm stuck with work. We all have to do some, so let's talk about how to get some, because a professional economist said it keeps getting harder to find some. (We know the economist is a pro because he kept pushing his glasses back up on his nose.) In fact, according to one report published by a leading economic firm (Bob's Leading Economic Firm, LLC), there are over 90 million Americans looking for work, but there are only eleven jobs available (and five of *those* are North Carolina poll watchers).

247

Okay. Technically, there are more than eleven jobs out there. (There are fifteen.) But they're not exactly the fairyland careers you dreamed of as a child. These are not "plum" positions. For example, I saw a plea from a publisher seeking contributions for a new anthology of "quality porn." I'm not sure exactly which discerning criteria are used to elevate *pedestrian* trash into *quality* trash; when it comes to porn, all I really know is this:

- It always contains characters who, no matter where they are at the time, think it's way too hot for all these clothes.
- Weird residential zoning rules require it to live hidden in a sock drawer, instead of displayed in a bookcase.
- Somewhere in each chapter, the author has to include the word "turgid."

Maybe, I thought, *quality* porn means *classic*. Timeless. Elevated, transcendent human meta-narratives, with the occasional swarthy Congressional page lobbed in to create tension. So I contacted the Quality Porn publisher and submitted a few candidate stories of my own:

- Of Inhuman Bondage
- Oliver's Twist
- Tess of the d'Urbervilles Pledges a Sorority
- Oedipus and the Terrible, Horrible, No Good, Very Bad Day
- Antony & Cleopatra & Ted & Alice
- Bleak Cat House

If I hear back from them, I'll let you know. Meanwhile, here are some other "Help Wanted" employment ads you might have seen recently, if I hadn't made them up:

- Wanted: Drivers to test-drive various Toyota models that have been rushed through a stupid federally-mandated recall, where repairs were completed by bitter Union laborers who just got back from smoking a joi ... uh, that is, who just got back from their lunch break. Ideal candidates will be unmarried risk-takers who, for whatever motives, have very little reason to continue living.

- Non-bony athlete needed to receive practice bites during the off-season. High pain threshold a plus. Good medical plan for the right candidate. Please contact "Cuspid" Suarez c/o the Uruguay Soccer Federation.

- Disturbed, narcissistic former Congressman seeks smart-phone assistant for taking anatomically-correct selfies. Ideal candidate will not think the name "Weiner" is a hilariously ironic coincidence.

- Hollywood director seeking scriptwriter for upcoming action-packed blockbuster, combining two of the most worn-out franchises in movie sequel history. Send writing samples to Transformers Die Hard XXVII: Would You Please Die Already And Take Some of These Decepticons With You

- Distracted nation seeks adult statesman with cogent foreign policy. Please forward golf handicap, all birth certificates, and any unsealed college transcripts to 1600 Pennsylvania Avenue.

Barry Parham

As you can see, there's work to be had, if you're a hard worker and don't mind minor inconveniences, like tetanus, or doing hard time. But these days, dedication and hard work come with another catch-22: if you work hard in America, you risk becoming <gasp> successful, which is the *last* thing you want to be in America...or at least, the last thing you want to *admit*. See, when you become a success, suddenly your internal body chemistry changes and you morph into a soulless, fanged racist who trips old people in the rain and makes house pets eat generic dry food from bags. In other words, by slipping up and letting yourself become successful, you have now become part of...

...the One Percent.

And once you're a One Percenter, you will be endlessly reviled by the mainstream media, and by posturing charlatans like that struggling, "flat broke" common laborer, Hillary Rodham Clinton, the poorest person you'll ever meet that pulls down $250,000 per speech, owns multiple homes, and has a net worth of $21.5 million.

And as the media condemn you and your sick, twisted, work-hard-and-make-something-out-of-yourself pathology, they'll do it with a condescending sneer, which is impressive, because it's hard to write words that sneer.

So be ready for it. They will hound you. They will snort and they will sniff.

Unless you're filthy poor. Like Hillary.

How Many is Nilnil?

Face paint, check. Funny hat, check. Catheter, check.

<><><>~~~~~~~~~~~~~~~~~~~~~~~~~~~<><><>

It happens every four years. Top-shelf athletes from countries across the globe gather, setting aside their border-based differences for a few perfect days to celebrate that purest, most cherished aspect of athletic competition: product endorsements.

As you probably figured out, we're talking about the World Cup, the only time European guys manage to run around in public for several hours without using their hands.

Americans call the game *soccer*, though the rest of the world calls it *futbol*. Of course, that sort of "you say *potato*, I say *spud*" thing happens a lot when comparing us to other nations. I mean, it's almost like those other countries have a different word for *everything*. For example, the leaders of many countries call themselves *king*, but America has Barack Obama, who calls himse ... okay, bad example.

Soccer works like this: each team is comprised of eleven guys -- ten sadists with multiple oversized hearts who *in utero* were already wearing cleats, and one mitt-wearing masochist (known as the *goalie*, or the *keeper*, or *that guy with no remaining convex facial features*). Both teams spend ninety non-stop minutes running up and down the field (the *pitch*) trying to kick a round ball into a mesh net (the *mesh net*), pausing every so often to fall down and try to win an Academy Award for acting injured. (*Best Feigned Agony Performance by a Non-Wounded Adult*)

Finally, when the game is over, the game isn't over. Some invisible official has randomly added several minutes to the clock, so the players have to stay on the field and *keep* running, while the coaches go find the timekeeper and slay him.

Actually, there are officials all over the place at your average soccer game, though nothing I've described so far would lead you to believe it. But during a soccer game, a player will occasionally do something particularly egregious, like use his hand, or suggest a red wine with fish. When this happens, a referee will put down the crossword puzzle he's been working, trot out to face the offending player, and hold up a red card (yellow if they're serving fish). The guilty player then performs the obligatory "Who, *ME?*" dance, like a Congressman caught in a public bathroom stall with a brick of tin-foiled money and three sheep dressed up as Penn State cheerleaders. Too many red and yellow cards, and the offender can get ejected from the game (unlike members of Congress). Then he has to go sit on the team bus and get gang-adored by fans.

If you're not familiar with futbol, it can admittedly sound like an odd sport. But then, we live on an odd planet, a place where fast food chains will take rib meat, cut out the rib bones, then machine-stamp the meat *to look like it still has ribs*, and customers buy the nasty things by the mcMillions.

And the world is full of candidates for "Most Psychotic Sport." In Afghanistan, tribesmen play a game called *buzkashi*, whenever they're not actively focused on turning all their women into Sylvia Plath. In a *buzkashi* match, which can last for several days, Afghanis on horseback basically race about slinging a dead goat at any nearby PETA evangelists. Not that *that's* a bad thing.

And speaking of odd sports -- in Mongolia and Tibet, the Mongs and the Tibs make a habit of racing yaks, which could be a humor column all by itself, but we really need to carom back to our original topic. (I just mentioned the yak racing to pester PETA.)

The first World Cup was held in 1930 and was hosted by Uruguay. (national motto: *Nobody exports more frozen bovine meat. Nobody.*) Uruguay is a South American country near Paraguay (literal translation: *two guays*). Sadly, though, only a handful of countries showed up for the first Cup, because it was a really long drive from Europe, and Al Gore still hadn't invented Frequent Flyer Miles.

Since 1930, the World Cup has been held every four years, except for a short break during World War II when FDR rationed Nike endorsements.

This year's competition is being hosted by Brazil, which is also called *Brasil*, but only by the people who live there. Russia will play host in 2018, assuming Vladimir Putin can find a shirt;

fours years after that, Qatar, a small Middle Eastern country paved about twelve miles deep in American money.

(For some reason, Qatar is variously pronounced *kotter*, *gutter*, and *ka-TAR*. But when you've got that kind of money, that's how things roll. By the time the 2022 World Cup rolls around, the country could be calling itself Sylvia.)

Meanwhile, in Brazil, the current World Cup is only about half over, so there's lots more *socfut* to see. And the games are not without their share of transnational drama, either; for example, the match between Switzerland and France, which almost didn't happen at all. At the coin toss, Switzerland refused to take a side. And then, during the Swiss national anthem, France surrendered to the band.

Then, in a nail-biter between Iran and Afghanistan, there was a slight delay when the Iranians brought a tactical nuclear warhead onto the pitch. But tensions subsided when Iran insisted the weapon would only be used to generate electricity.

But no matter where the World Cup is played, or how many ways people misspell *football*, it's simply gonna take some time for Americans to adjust to it all.

Here's a perfect example: during the match between Honduras and Ecuador, Honduras scored...*and nobody cut to a commercial.* Then, almost immediately, Ecuador scored. And still, *no commercial break.*

Weird. How do *futbol* fans ever decide which car to buy?

Abnormal is Other People

"We have nothing to phobe but phobe itself."

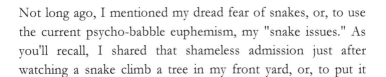

Not long ago, I mentioned my dread fear of snakes, or, to use the current psycho-babble euphemism, my "snake issues." As you'll recall, I shared that shameless admission just after watching a snake climb a tree in my front yard, or, to put it more calmly, after seeing a "mind-scarring vision from deepest hell."

Scientists don't say "fear," of course - they've coined their own word to describe such intense uncomfortable with-edness. Scientists prefer *phobia* rather than fear, presumably because phobia has way more syllables, and syllable count is important when you're padding a thesis, or tap-dancing for a government grant. (*source: the International Scientist Handbook For Effective Grant-Grabbing*)

And so, scientists and psycho-babble professionals can now take anybody's petrifying fear and just sling the suffix *-phobia* at it, which makes it immediately eligible for taxpayer-funded research. (*source: the Congressional Insider's Guide To Earmarks That Are Critical To National Security, Nudge-Nudge Wink-Wink*)

255

Interestingly, scientists have come up with several syllable-rich tags for my particular shriek-inducing fear, fear of snakes - there's *Ophidiophobia* and *Ophiophobia*, both of which refer to an "abnormal" fear of snakes, as if there was such a thing...as if it's somehow "abnormal" to shun a fell creature that carries around two poison-packed hypos in its mouth. And then there's *Herpetophobia*, a more general fear of reptiles and amphibians. (as opposed to *Herpesophobia*: the fear of being soul-kissed by Madonna)

Like many hard-to-spell terms, the word ophidiophobia comes from the Greeks: a combination of *phobia*, meaning "fear," and *ophis*, meaning "sick, unholy beast that slithers, has fangs, and even though it doesn't have hands or feet can climb trees, for Pete's sake, which is just wrong." (*source: the International Coalition Of Anti-Reptile Sane People, Which Doesn't Actually Exist, But Should*)

Also, according to the internet, care must be taken to differentiate between ophidiophobes and people who just occasionally don't like snakes. A snake-o-phobe would not only fear live snakes, but snakes in pictures, snakes on TV, snakes in anecdotes, plumber's snakes, 'snake' used as a verb, and so on.

Touché. Guilty as charged. Back in the '80s, I almost refused to buy a Wang Chung album because one of the tracks was named "Snake Dance."

It turns out that, as I go through my life staring out windows, sweating and cursing mildly while snakes scale trees, I have plenty of company. About a third of the people on Earth are herpetophobic, which by a strange coincidence is also the number of people Madonna has dated. (*source: Sean Penn*)

And in case you're standing there reading this, thinking, "What a wimp!," I have three responses:

- There are lots of phobias out there more bizarre than mine
- Next time you walk to your mailbox, be sure to check the trees
- You gotta try *way* harder than a simple "wimp" to insult *me*. I work with people in Marketing. I've been insulted by the *best*.

So. While you're busy trying to ignore those odd thumping sounds under the trees in your yard, here are some other phobias you might want to consider getting, from a list compiled by the experts, except for the ones I made up. (*source: he International Council That Catalogs Phobias, Irrational Fears, And Other Selling Tools Used By Politicians*)

Ablutophobia
Fear of bathing

Blutophobia
Fear of John Belushi in "Animal House"

Ablutoblutophobia
Fear of bathing with John Belushi

Caligynephobia

Fear of beautiful women

Gynophobia
Fear of OB/GYNs

Caligynophobia
Fear of beautiful OB/GYNs

Blutogynophobia
Fear of finding out your OB/GYN is John Belushi

Ephebiphobia
Fear of teenagers

Adulthood
Fear of teenagers

Spectrophobia
Fear of looking at one's own reflection in a mirror

Spectrodraculaphobia
Fear of looking at one's own reflection in a mirror and not seeing anything

Spectrodracostokerphobia
Fear of not seeing your reflection in the mirror and then being hunted down by local villagers and staked in the heart

Scopophobia
Fear of being seen or stared at

Scopospectrophobia

Fear of looking in the mirror and seeing yourself looking at yourself in the mirror

Triskaidekaphobia
Fear of the number 13

Trickadickaphobia
Fear of Richard Nixon

Friggatriskaidekaphobia
Fear of Friday the 13th

Friggabuffalophobia
Fear of chicken wing appetizers from TGI Friday's

Chrometophobia
Fear of money

Prenuptophobia
Fear of not having money

Liberalism
Fear of not having other people's money

Chorophobia
Fear of dancing

Chorovideophobia
Fear of "Dancing with the Stars"

Peladophobia
Fear of bald people

Peladochorophobia
Fear of dancing with bald people

Arachibutyrophobia
Fear of having peanut butter stick to the roof of your mouth

Peladobutyrophobia
Fear of having bald people stick to the roof of your mouth

Papaphobia
Fear of the Pope

Papapeladophobia
Fear of bald Popes

Papaspectropeladotriskaphobia
Fear of looking in the mirror and seeing thirteen bald Popes

Papawasarollingstonophobia
Fear of Motown

Nomophobia
Fear of being away from your smartphone

Nomopapaphobia
Fear of being away from your smartphone when the Pope calls

Nomoverizonswapophobia
Fear of having an outdated smartphone but you can't upgrade until next November because you're locked in to a stupid contract

Liberalism
Fear of having to pay for your own smartphone

~-~-~-~-~-~-~-~-~-~-~

 So, remember, as you enjoy your well-kempt suburban lawn and dodge paratrooper snakes - be nice to people. Everybody's lugging their own little valise of private terror.

And be thankful. You could've been saddled with the trickiest phobia of them all: Phobophobia.

Yep. You guessed it. Fear of fear itself.

(source: the Secret Vatican Archives of Pope Roosevelt XIII)

Barry Parham

Abe Lincoln, Rabbi

History, no. Lunch, yes.

<><><>~~~~~~~~~~~~~~~~~~~~~~~~~<><><>

Watch your back, everybody. These are dangerous days, and the black helicopters are everywhere. Conspiracies, thick as thieves, roil in the streets, and none more dire than this one out of Texas: in Dallas, a conspiracy museum has been killed.

By a Quiznos.

"Yeah, right," you say, assuming you're the type of person who argues with humor columns. "You blame the sandwich shop for taking out the museum? Well, I happen to know better. Quiznos was with *me* that night. We was playing poker with Schlotzsky's."

In case you didn't know – and based on their ranking among Texas tourist attractions, you didn't – the Dallas Conspiracy Museum, which opened in 1995, has now mysteriously closed. Odder still, some claim it's only closed...temporarily. (Actually, it closed in December 2006, but it was just last week that anybody noticed.) Was there a conspiracy to close the

Conspiracy Museum? No one's certain, but very few persistently paranoid people are buying the official statement from the museum's president, Tom Bowden, who offered only this cryptic comment:

"Basically, they're putting a Quiznos here."

Right. A sub shop. Certainly. I bet they won't really sell any food. I smell CIA front.

~-~-~-~-~-~-~-~-~-~-~-~

Culinary Sidebar: I assume Quiznos was founded by somebody named Quiznos. With a name like that, what else could he do? Open a law practice? Would *you* retain attorneys from Quiznos, Berkowitz, & Quiznos LLC?

Some career choices are simply thrust upon you. For example, that jelly guy, Smuckers. Or Orville Redenbacher. What were Orville's options? Fine jewelry?

~-~-~-~-~-~-~-~-~-~-~-~

The now-shuttered Conspiracy Museum was founded by one R.B. Cutler, who bills himself as an "assassinologist," a word which, like the museum's vast commercial success, doesn't exist. The headliner at the Dallas Conspiracy Museum, of course, is the conspiracy around who *really* shot JFK in 1963, just down the street from this recently established, shifty-looking Quiznos. Most people think the shooter was a man named Lee Harvey Oswald, but a handful of people want to lay the blame elsewhere. You can usually recognize these conspiracy types by the way they walk around arguing loudly with invisible people.

~-~-~-~-~-~-~-~-~-~-~

Historical Sidebar: John (*Jack*) Fitzgerald (*Gatsby*) Kennedy (*JFK*) was America's 35th President (*P35*), as every American schoolchild knows, assuming somebody texted it to them (*OMG LOL*). President Kennedy was best known for two things: making Nikita Khrushchev get off Ricky Ricardo's porch, and sex. JFK had staggering amounts of sex, or as Warren Beatty would put it, not very much sex. According to Presidential historians, JFK was often, um, visited, by actress Marilyn Monroe, who used to bring him, um, pizzas.

Thanks to JFK, having lots of sex while at work became a pattern that would be picked up by future Democrat Presidents, except for Barack Obama, who preferred golf, and if you've seen his wife, you'd putt, too. (Instead, he appointed a Czar to have huge amounts of proxy sex without Congressional approval. When Obama announced he was hiring a Sex Czar, he was nearly crushed to death by job applicants.)

~-~-~-~-~-~-~-~-~-~-~

However, Cutler's Conspiracy Museum didn't stop with just the JFK intrigue. The former tourist unattraction also offered exhibits analyzing the assassinations of Abraham Lincoln, Martin Luther King, Bobby Kennedy, and Cutler even took a conspiratorial swipe at Ted Kennedy's Chappaquiddick incident. The assassinologist argued that all these conspiracies...all of them, mind you – from Abe Lincoln to Ted Kennedy...all of them could be tied together in one great, big conspiratorial web, which proves that Cutler is not only an assassinologist, but a crazyologist, too.

Coincidentally (or not), the Dallas Conspiracy Museum is just down the street from the Dallas Holocaust Museum, and it turns out there are actually *four* Holocaust Museums in Texas. Not that there's anything wrong with that, of course, but when I ponder Israel's long rich history, there's not a lot of references to Texas. On the other hand, with a name like Abraham, maybe President Lincoln was Jewish. I think Cutler and Quiznos should look into it.

But leading the field in the Most Paranoid Conspiracies Challenge has to be this one: the Conspiracy Museum's straight-faced theory that there were *two* Lee Harvey Oswalds. Not to worry – we can immediately debunk that nonsense, thanks to the fact-filled novel *11/22/63*, penned by famous horrorologist Stephen King, in which somebody travelled back in time by walking down some invisible steps in the back corner of a diner's pantry, in order to stop both Oswalds from killing Kennedy, attend Abe Lincoln's circumcision, and to give Khrushchev a wedgie.

And keep in mind that it's not a good idea to argue with Stephen King. Get on *his* bad side, and he could write you in to his next book, and then kill you.

Twice.

Winding Down Civilization
Vote for your what?

<><><>~~~~~~~~~~~~~~~~~~~~~~~~~<><><>

I didn't believe it at first. When my friend sent me the link, I thought, "Nah. No way a planet would do that to itself." But I checked it out, and it's true. You can now buy a doll that looks like a politician.

This is a major breakthrough. Back in the day, we had to buy the whole politician.

And, of course, the best thing about buying a politician doll is, if the *doll* sucks at its job, you can return it.

Actually, you can shop several competing versions of several politician dolls. Maybe there'll need to be a runoff. Plastic primaries between die-cast candidates.

Wait...we do that *now*.

At the acme of the current pol doll pantheon, of course, is the Barack Obama Poseable Talking Doll (teleprompters sold separately). According to their website (Dysfunctional-

Geppetto-Caucus.com), the Barack Obama Poseable Talking Doll recites dozens of disjointed buzzwords and scripted insincere inspirational phrases - just like Obama himself.

But that's just for starters! The doll-in-chief that thinks America has fifty-seven States is packed with lots of *other* crowd-pleasing features, too!

- Deluxe auto-grin feature!
- Patented "pivot like a laser" agenda generator!
- can reproduce all of Obama's rhetorical hand gestures, including the ever-popular "up-and-down pointy shapes with his thumb and forefinger"
- fully poseable; includes handy "how-to" protocols showing the proper way to bow down before foreign leaders
- package contains a custom doll stand, with a little stick that you shove up his posterity
- exemption vouchers available for Union members and some 2,000 other sketchily-defined groups (just not *you*)
- package includes a blank sheet of paper - create your own foreign policy! (please)
- comes with several birth certificates of authority from various countries
- completely programmable; can be operated by remote control (George Soros sold separately)

Another favorite figurine of late is the Barack Obama action figure, brought to you by -- I am not good enough to make this stuff up -- Jailbreak Toys. We're not sure where they got the design specs for an action figure, because nobody I've talked to has ever *seen* Obama in action.

Well, you can't blame the *marketers*. I imagine it'd be tough during the holiday shopping season to try and get shoppers excited over a "lack of action figure."

Of course, it does beg the question: if I like the action figures I already have, can I keep them?

But the good folks at Jailbreak are apparently big Obama fans -- though maybe not the world's best proofreaders. In a breathless quote that could easily have been penned by tingly news anchors at MSNBC, here's how they described that magic moment in 2008 when President Obama was elected:

" He was the closet thing to a living, breathing superhero we'd ever seen..."

Yes, that is a direct quote. But I'm not sure which reference is more disturbing; the "superhero" part or the "closet" part.

No matter. I've learned that sometimes you just have to let the joke go...especially when the butt of the joke has an army.

So let's move on.

Because this is America, land of the "Free! You just pay shipping!" scam and home of the velvet Elvis, you can also buy a Barack Obama-themed doll marketed as "The Pootin' Tootin' President." I won't go into the product's details, other than to point out that the doll's signature attraction occurs when you pull the doll's finger.

Ah, civilization. Literature. Art. Music. The Big Gulp and the bottomless salad. And now, the Pootin' POTUS. Ah, well. Could be worse, I suppose. There could be a Russian version...the Pootin' Putin.

And along those lines, here are some other themed dolls that are available...or should be:

- the Mayor Bloomberg doll: pull its string and your soda disappears
- the Dianne Feinstein doll: pull its string and your gun disappears
- the Al Sharpton doll: pull its string and Tawana Brawley disappears
- the Eric Holder doll: pull its string and it has you arrested (legal justification not included)
- the Bill Clinton doll: pull its string and it feels your pain, or whatever else you got (spot remover not included)
- the Andrew Weiner doll: Hey, that's not a string!
- the Michelle Obama doll: pull its string and it boards a plane, flies away on vacation, and then complains about never getting a vacation (actual cost to the American taxpayer not included)
- the Mitch McConnell doll: when you pull its string, it makes all the right noises, but it's not really what it says it is

- the Dennis Rodman doll: pull its string and marries itself. As a bonus, the doll's head and neck are cleverly designed as a place to store all your jewelry!
- the Harry Reid doll: pull its string and it talks, but nobody has a clue what it's saying (includes cents-off coupon for Whack-a-Koch Brother arcade game)
- the Jay Carney parrot doll: now with Private Sector smirks!
- Henri, the Parisian doll: pull its string and it insults you. And then it surrenders. (not available in August)
- the John Boehner doll: a clumsy, tangerine-colored doll that repeatedly paints the other dolls into a corner. Pull its string and it cries.
- the Kim Jong-un doll: the perfect playmate for your Dennis Rodman doll - and at 8" tall, the little Kim doll is life-size!
- the Hillary Clinton doll: you can pull its string all you want; it's still gonna refuse to talk (reason for existence not included)
- the South Africa Interpreter doll: pull its string and it translates whatever you say into complete gibberish
- the John Kerry doll: pull its string and it asks its wife what to say
- the Willie Nelson doll: smokes the string
- the Sean Penn doll: pull its string and it demands you sign its petition for world peace. Refuse and it punches you in the face. (assault & batteries not included)
- the Nancy Pelosi doll: finally...a *Mrs.* Potato Head. (votes sold separately)

One final note: there's also a Joe Biden doll out there, but the manufacturer recommends you remove the little string that makes *him* talk.

Period.

Quickly.

Hair of the Corn Dog

"I rewrite the songs that make the whol..."

Sometimes a news story comes along that so perfectly encapsulates the overarching beauty - and the pain - of Earthly existence, a story that so enriches the collective human experience, a humor columnist has to take a solemn pause to share it with his readers.

This is not one of those days.

On the other hand, every now and again the news delivers such a You-Gotta-Be-Kiddin-Me headline that any non-medicated humorist could pretty much just reheat it, rewrap it, and resell it to the next car in the drive-thru. Witness:

A 60-year-old man arrested for DUI outside a store in Georgia told the arresting officer that his dog drove him to the store to buy some corn.

See what I mean? A story like that -- it's an absolute gift for somebody writing a humor column. I mean, I'm a half-dozen paragraphs in and I still haven't had to make anything up.

According to the police report, the tale began when a local sheriff responded to a call about an alleged dog allegedly locked in a car. (Somehow, the dog had managed to get its driver's license, but apparently missed "How To Unlock the Door" day.) The officer proceeded, both allegedly and cautiously, to Bell's Alleged Food, the only grocery I've ever seen that got a one-star review. (To be fair, the reviewer misspelled *twice*. And *gross*. Twicet.)

According to the news report, Bell's is located down the street from the Chicken Express off Experiment Station Road, just past the new stop light at Hog Mountain Road, and we all knew a Hog Mountain Road would turn up somewhere in this story.

(When we zoom out the map, we learn that this canine crime scene was situated somewhere in Oconee County, just south of Athens, which is home to the University of Georgia (my alma mater). This is not really relevant to *this* crime story, but if you follow Georgia football, you know that anytime anybody gets arrested for DUI within 100 miles of Athens, the coaches get nervous.)

Outside the store, reported the sheriff, it was a balmy 99-degree day, but the internal temperature of the alleged car was 123 degrees. (We're assuming the dog unlocked the door for the cop, after asking to see some ID.)

When the sheriff identified and confronted the alleged dog's alleged owner, the 60-year-old immediately outlined his innocence. He claimed he and the family cat had been minding their own business at home, passed out in the garage after an overly liquor-laced night at Eulene's All-You-Can-Eat Potted Meat Buffet & Karaoke Parlor, when the dog leapt in the driver's seat, sucker-punched the cat, raced to the store, and demanded corn in a baying and completely un-Southern Baptist tone of voice.

Ultimately, the alleged cat burglar was charged with animal cruelty, driving under the influence, and being criminally stupid within 200 feet of a Hog Mountain Road. This means the 60-year-old now has a criminal record, which makes him immediately eligible as a defensive back for the Georgia Bulldogs. (the technical term is "redshirt freshman")

It's unclear what happened to the dog. Locals say it was likely spirited away into Animal Control's custody, although it's entirely possible the little pound-dodger's getaway car skills were spotted by local NASCAR scouts.

But a news blurb like this does lend itself to a quick round of...

Potential Newspaper Headlines

MAN & DOG NABBED IN D.U.I. STING; DOG PLEADS FIFTH BEFORE MAN CAN DRINK IT

DOG ARRESTED FOR FAILING TO SIGNAL LEFT TURN; ASPCA ATTORNEY MOUNTS "NO OPPOSABLE THUMBS" DEFENSE

CAR IMPOUNDED, GETAWAY DRIVER DOGPOUNDED

Barry Parham

DESPERATE MAN THROWS DOG UNDER BUS; DISGRUNTLED POOCH CLAIMS OWNER STILL NOT HOUSETRAINED

GEORGIA MAN WAVES GOODBYE TO FAVORITE HOUND AS PRISON DOORS SLAM SHUT; 10,000 COUNTRY MUSIC SINGERS SIMULTANEOUSLY STRUM E-MINOR

ACCOMPLICE NABBED AFTER LEAVING LEASH AT CRIME SCENE

ENTIRE UNIV OF GA OFFENSE IMPRISONED IN SPAM BUFFET INCIDENT ON HOG MT. ROAD; UNIV PR DEPT TESTS NEW MOTTO: "HERE AT UGA, ORANGE IS THE NEW RED & BLACK"

MAN & ALLEGORICAL BEST FRIEND ARRESTED; DOG REQUESTS SEPARATE LEGAL COUNSEL

DOG BUYS CORN; CORN LURES MAN; MAN BECOMES PRESIDENT; PRESIDENT EATS DOG; THOUSANDS KILLED IN GALACTIC-LEVEL IRONY OVERLOAD

GUNS DISCHARGED DURING ARREST: ACLU CLAIMS OFFICER OVER-REACTED TO BEING SNIFFED

HOLLYWOOD STUDIO BUYS RIGHTS TO ROGUE DOG'S ORDEAL; PUP IMMEDIATELY CONTACTED BY CELEBRITY ATTORNEY GLORIA ALLRED

276

PAROLE BOARD DENIES EARLY RELEASE FOLLOWING BIZARRE LEG-HUMPING INCIDENT. TWICET.

CAT TURNS STATE'S EVIDENCE

Barry Parham

###

About the Author

Barry Parham is a recovering software freelancer and the author of humor columns, essays and short stories. He is a music fanatic and a 1981 honors graduate of the University of Georgia.

Writing awards and recognitions earned by Parham include taking First Place in the November 2009 Writer's Circle Competition, First Prize in the March 2012 writing contest at HumorPress.com, and a plug by the official website of the Erma Bombeck Writers' Workshop. Most recently, Parham's work has appeared in four national humor anthologies.

Author's website
http://www.barryparham.com

@ facebook
http://www.facebook.com/pmWriter

@ Twitter
http://twitter.com/barryparham

@ Google+
http://tinyurl.com/n6w5gq4

Barry Parham